"Doug Stephens sounds the alarm for brick-and-mortar retailers; those who do not heed his advice do so at their own peril. *Reengineering Retail* is a survival guide for those navigating a sea change in physical retail."

••••••• **MARK TORO**, Founder and Managing Partner,
North American Properties–Atlanta, Ltd.

"Disruption is facing every business. Retail is feeling the brunt of it. Software eats retail in a one-click and swipe-right world. Retailers talk about omnichannel and customer-centricity, but look at the landscape: it's hard to be optimistic. Big thinkers like Doug Stephens and his latest book, *Reengineering Retail*, demonstrate what retailers need to think and do in this landscape. If you sell stuff, this is a must-read."

••••••• **MITCH JOEL**, President of Mirum and
author of *Six Pixels of Separation* and *Ctrl Alt Delete*

"Ten years ago, walking into a cool boutique to see a DJ spinning was novel. Today, it's about the least a store can do to keep up. Brands and retailers that stand out are pulling out the stops to turn shopping into a rich, immersive experience that leverages technology. Doug's book demonstrates how to best compete in this new retail world."

••••••• **HARLEY FINKELSTEIN**, Chief Operating Officer, Shopify

"Doug Stephens paints a vivid picture of the massive disruption and reinvention that is occurring in retail. *Reengineering Retail* offers valuable insights into how the physical and the digital retailing worlds will combine to create customer experiences we can only imagine today. This book is a wake-up call to any retailers that have been technological laggards."

••••••• **RAMESH VENKAT**, Ph.D., Director, David Sobey Centre
for Innovation in Retailing, Saint Mary's University

"Doug Stephens' latest book, *Reengineering Retail*, shines the spotlight on the new retail ecosystem, one that feeds off innovation, the redefinition of customer experience, authenticity, value, excitement and experimentation. Doug's book challenges us to look at disruption more than by assuming that one form of retail will win over another—the book forces us to understand the power of personalization and customer engagement—the lifeblood of our new retail world."

••••••• **DIANE J. BRISEBOIS**, President and CEO, Retail Council of Canada

DOUG STEPHENS

Foreword by **Joseph Pine**

REENGINEERING RETAIL

The Future of Selling in a Post-Digital World

Figure.1
Vancouver / Berkeley

Copyright © 2017 by Doug Stephens
Foreword © 2017 by B. Joseph Pine II

17 18 19 20 21   5 4 3

Cataloguing data is available from Library and Archives Canada
ISBN 978-1-927958-81-0 (hbk.)
ISBN 978-1-927958-80-3 (ebook)
ISBN 978-1-927958-96-4 (pdf)

Design by Jessica Sullivan
Author photograph by Retail Prophet

Editing by Diana Byron
Copy editing by Lucy Kenward
Proofreading by Melanie Little
Indexing by Sergey Lobachev

Printed and bound in Canada by Friesens
Distributed in the U.S. by Publishers Group West

Figure 1 Publishing Inc.
Vancouver BC Canada
www.figure1pub.com

Dedicated to all those who keep
their heads in the clouds and
their feet off the ground,
those with the courage to defy
the voices of reason.

Contents

Foreword

TWO GREAT FORCES flow across the economic landscape.

The first is the *commoditization* of goods and services, for people increasingly want to buy them at the greatest possible convenience and the lowest possible price. The rise of the Internet as a platform for purchasing exacerbates this force. People can instantly compare prices from one vendor to another, which tends to push them down to the lowest possible price. Or forget the price comparison—just go to Amazon.com where you're assured a great (if not the lowest) price and even greater convenience: one click, boom, done, your purchase is heading to your home!

The second great force is the shift into the Experience Economy. Goods and services are no longer enough; people increasingly desire *experiences*—memorable events that engage each individual in an inherently personal way. We see this fundamental shift in the very fabric of the economy in the rise of theme parks, theme restaurants, boutique hotels, and of course experiential retail, where cafés, pop-up stores, showrooms, climbing walls, yoga studios, and countless other experiences engage consumers in retail stores. Surprisingly, manufacturers are making most of these innovations, not retailers themselves!

And naturally these forces intertwine. Consumers *want* goods and services to be commoditized so they can spend their hard-earned money, and their harder-earned time, on the experiences they value so much more highly.

Retail expert Doug Stephens lays out the stark choice retailers have in the face of these forces: create innovative experiences or be commoditized. Providing a tour of what is being done now and what is possible in the future, Doug lays out a roadmap that you can follow in determining what the store of the future should be—for you. In doing so, he hits on some points near and dear to my own heart.

Doug's exactly right in saying that we need to understand that "The Store Is Media," or as I like to put it, the experience *is* the marketing. The best way to generate demand for your retail offerings is through an experience so engaging that consumers can't help but spend time in your place, give you their attention, and buy your offerings as a result.

Doug beautifully defines remarkable experiences as those that are *engaging, unique, personalized, surprising,* and *repeatable*. How can you design and stage a store experience that fits those five adjectives? Read here to figure that out.

That third adjective, "personalized," is incredibly important, as Doug highlights with the possibilities for mass-customizing offerings within (and without) your retail venues, particularly thanks to the rise of 3D printing. Even if that particular digital technology doesn't make sense for your business, do recognize that experiences are inherently personal. They actually happen *inside* people in reaction to the events and places you stage for them. Therefore, the more personal you make your experiences, and your retail offerings, the more engaging and memorable you will be.

And best of all, Doug encourages you to conquer your fear of all the various digital technologies that so often keep consumers out of physical stores, and he shows you how to embrace them to enhance your in-store experience. You need not dread online buying once you understand that Reality will now and forevermore provide the richest of experiences—especially since that richness can be enhanced through technologies that enable you to *fuse* the real and the virtual.

Let *Reengineering Retail* be your guide in today's increasingly turbulent world of retail, for again you must make your choice: stage retail experiences or be commoditized.

B. JOSEPH PINE II
Dellwood, Minnesota
Co-founder, Strategic Horizons LLP
Co-author, *The Experience Economy* and *Infinite Possibility: Creating Customer Value on the Digital Frontier*

RETAIL IS DEAD

Software
Eats Retail

"SOFTWARE EATS RETAIL." This was technology investor Marc Andreessen's morbid epitaph for the retail industry in a January 2013 interview. Andreessen, the co-founder of the web browser Netscape Navigator, is also one of Silicon Valley's most influential investment gurus and one-half of the eponymous venture capital powerhouse Andreessen Horowitz. His company has interests in an array of Internet technology firms, including Facebook, Airbnb, Twitter and Pinterest, to name only a few. He also sits on the boards of Facebook and Hewlett-Packard and has spent decades as a technology practitioner, innovator, investor and advisor, triangulating the future of the web and betting big on what he sees coming next. Moreover, he has a reputation for doing so with alarming acuity. Consequently, when he clears his throat to speak, people tend to sit up and listen, hoping to catch even a momentary glimpse into his deadly accurate crystal ball.

Not one to mince words, he summed up his industry outlook by saying, "Retail guys are going to go out of business and ecommerce will become the place everyone buys....Retail chains are a fundamentally implausible economic structure if there's a viable alternative. You combine the fixed cost of real estate with inventory, and it puts every retailer in a highly leveraged position. Few can survive a decline of 20 to 30 percent in revenues. It just doesn't make any sense for all this stuff to sit on shelves. There is fundamentally a better model."[1]

Mic drop.

The interview had barely pixelated on Twitter before sparking a firestorm of debate. Industry analysts, pundits and even retail executives themselves began offering up ammunition on both sides of the argument.

Some felt that Andreessen's comments were utter bullshit and not much more than the bluster of an investor with an obvious and vested financial axe to grind on behalf of the technology companies he was so deeply involved with. They pointed to the impossibility of a retail world without "retail guys," as Andreessen called them. They decried pure-play online retail as a failed business model being propped up by endless streams of venture capital that, in the end, would collapse under its own weight.

Others took a very different view, falling in line behind him and pointing to the disastrous impact of technology on other verticals, such as the brick-and-mortar travel industry— an industry that had been all but laid to waste by online travel options. They pointed to the downfall of businesses like Blockbuster, which once held almost 30 percent market share in the video rental market and yet was wiped off the face of the Earth by Netflix and video on demand in little more than a decade. They called out the retail industry incumbents for their failure to meet the pace of progress around them.

To their point, within a little more than two hundred years we've witnessed the following technological innovations become things we simply take for granted.

→ the lightbulb
→ the telegraph
→ the electromagnet
→ petroleum
→ the telephone
→ the vacuum tube
→ semiconductors
→ penicillin
→ the radio
→ the electron
→ quantum physics
→ the airplane
→ television
→ the transistor
→ the discovery of DNA
→ the integrated circuit
→ the Internet
→ microprocessors
→ the mobile phone
→ the smartphone
→ the quantum computer

Technological progress and its impact on humanity has been staggering. How many of us could possibly imagine a world without these things? And yet, in the face of all of this, the concept of retail and how it's carried out hasn't changed much at all. The way we go to the store, browse products and pay for those products is essentially the same today as it was two hundred years ago. Sure, we don't use a horse and buggy to deliver goods anymore and cash registers don't have bells, but the core economic model for how retailers buy products and sell those products to consumers is the same in almost every respect as it was in the mid-1800s. Those in Andreessen's camp were right to wonder, how could retail possibly be so out of sync with progress on most other fronts?

I decided to take a somewhat less passionate approach to the debate. After all, I had no dog in this fight, and it felt to me that there were merits and flaws in both arguments.

First, the pundits and analysts of today pointing to pure-play online retail as an emperor without any clothes sounded oddly reminiscent of the voices that dissented when Bill Gates dreamed that one day there would be "a computer on every desk in every home." They were skeptics who cited what was obvious at the time: that computers were onerously complex and costly. However, they, like most naysayers throughout history, were mired in parochial thinking and overlooked the combinatorial and exponential nature of innovation. The cost of computers, of course, has dropped precipitously, and they can now be used by toddlers without instruction—something Gates clearly foresaw, but that completely eluded many of his critics.

Similarly short-sighted, the former head of Blockbuster, John Antioco, suggested in 2000 that Netflix was destined to remain a "very small niche business." At the time, of course, he was right. Netflix was a comparatively small mail-order video business with less than 10 percent market share. What Antioco missed, however, was the exponential potential for streaming entertainment that would turn Netflix from a minor distraction into a catastrophic disruption. To suggest that pure-play online retail is unsustainable based on a quarterly report from Amazon today would be no less myopic or near-sighted.

On the other hand, it also seemed to me that to suggest a future absent of any physical retail was to negate the human essence of shopping and reduce it to a passionless matter of mere product acquisition. And suggesting that "ecommerce will become the place that everyone buys" sounded eerily like analysts' predictions for big-box retail two decades ago, when they characterized it as an unstoppable business model. Yet today, big-box retail is coming apart at the seams. Was it not conceivable that a similar fate could await today's online incumbents?

So what was the truth? Beyond the hyperbole and the binary predictions on both sides, where *was* retail headed? What would the "store" of the future really look like, and how could retailers across the spectrum adapt and survive what was coming?

This is what I set out to understand.

What I have discovered is that what lies ahead is infinitely more amazing than we could have imagined. Every aspect of how, where, when and even why we shop is about to change entirely. Online or offline—retail is on the precipice of a historic reinvention that will leave both digital and physical retail barely recognizable in comparison to the way we shop today. Even the centuries-old formula through which retail companies make money—the core economic model—is going to be shape-shifted beyond recognition and with it, the very concept of what a store *is* and what it *does* is going to be rewritten.

Marc Andreessen was right that January day. Retail was indeed going to crash and burn. But out of its smoldering ashes an entirely new and amazing industry was about to be born.

Farewell
to Bentonville

IT'S HARD TO fully appreciate Walmart until you've made a pilgrimage to the quaint southeastern U.S. town of Bentonville, Arkansas. In 2015, I headed there to deliver a presentation on the future of retail to the company's executives.

Bentonville may as well be called Walmartville because frankly, were it not for Walmart, I'm not sure one could find Bentonville on a map. Its hotels, shops, restaurants and taxi services exist primarily to serve Walmart and the endless stream of businesspeople who come and go at the company's behest. There's even a Walmart museum housed inside the original Walton's 5&10 store. It's a surreal walk through time that includes photos and memorabilia chronicling the company's growth. There are original 1960s-era products and even a completely intact replica of Sam Walton's original office, down to the memos that sat on his desk. I imagine there was a time, not long ago, when this museum must have stood as a victorious tribute to Walmart's dominance. When I visited in 2015, however, the

The Walmart Museum in Bentonville, Arkansas.

experience struck me as oddly sad, sort of like the meticulously maintained trophy case of an over-the-hill high school athlete trying desperately to relive the glory days.

But what glory days they were. Between 1962 and 2010 the chain opened an astonishing 4,393 stores across America, with more than 3,000 of those opening post-1990. Their growth both domestically and abroad was simply unprecedented. Under the watchful eye of its charismatic founder, Sam Walton, Walmart became the world's largest and most dominant retailer, and in doing so completely reshaped the entire retail industry. In its heyday, just about anyone you spoke to worked for, sold to or competed with Walmart. Walmart, it seemed, *was* retail.

Success, however, can also become one's worst enemy, and by the late 2000s it was apparent that many of the trappings of

Walmart's former greatness had become the very things threatening its success. Its enormous, big-box footprint seemed out of step with a new era of more considered consumption. Its labor practices, once hailed, were now under the constant scrutiny of advocacy groups and unions. Its commitments to domestic sourcing were questioned, and its in-store experience was, by most accounts, leaving much to be desired. All of this weighed heavily on the retailer's sales results, which became uncharacteristically flat.

Furthermore, where Walmart had once dominated the low end of the price spectrum, a new army of competitors—including dollar stores and off-price outlet malls—was now undercutting it. In fact, in 2007, as though publicly acknowledging this new market reality, Walmart changed its immortal brand slogan from "Always Low Prices" to a new and decidedly more equivocal, "Save Money. Live Better."

Only a year later, however, Walmart's core customers were not living better. In fact, they were among the hardest hit by the worst recession in history and began venturing to wherever the best deal was to be had. Increasingly, it wouldn't be found at Walmart.

In the meantime, another weakness made itself glaringly apparent. Walmart had largely missed the entire digital retail movement. While it had experimented with online sales in the late 1990s, most efforts to evolve its capabilities were sidelined in favor of riding the wave of growth in its physical store business. By the late 2000s, however, it became increasingly clear that consumers were moving online in droves, and Walmart hadn't moved with them.

In 2012, Walmart's revenues were sixteen times those of Amazon, making it somewhat easier to dismiss the e-tailer as a profitless nuisance. Only four years later, however, Amazon had shrunk that to a mere five times and was rapidly closing the gap. Moreover, Amazon's revenue per employee in 2015, $623,000 according to *Time* magazine, was three times that of Walmart.

Also in 2015, something happened that would have seemed inconceivable only a decade earlier. Walmart suffered its first sales decline ever—at least since the company went public forty-five years prior.[1] For many companies a loss of this kind wouldn't have signified crisis. For Walmart it was a cataclysm. The mythic company that only a decade earlier had put its competitors into a cold sweat was now itself backed into a corner, coming under attack from all sides. The retailer that had spent fifty years breaking records was now, seemingly, the one being broken.

But what must have been the bitterest pill to swallow also came later the same year, when Amazon surged ahead to unseat Walmart as the world's most valuable retailer. Amazon's market capitalization had passed the $250 billion mark, exceeding Walmart's value by $20 billion. In only two decades, Jeff Bezos had built a company worth more—on paper at least—than the one Sam Walton and his heirs spent more than fifty years constructing.

While Walmart pointed a finger at what it saw as predatory pricing on Amazon's part, what became clear was that the root of its weakness had much less to do with price and more to do with selection. In 2015, Walmart.com carried 11 million products, a mere 4 percent of the 260 million products carried on Amazon.com.[2] Walmart, the retailer that once dwarfed all others with its footprint, was now the one being made to look small.

Adding insult to injury, Amazon was also thrashing Walmart in the one sacrosanct metric that brick-and-mortar retailers had considered their sole dominion—customer service. Amazon was consistently killing Walmart and most other physical retailers in customer satisfaction surveys, often coming in at the very top of the field.

Walmart goes shopping

The gravity of all of this was by no means eluding Walmart. In fact, as far back as 2012 the company had already begun desperately attempting to catch up to its online rivals. That year Walmart made a decisive investment in that effort with the $300 million acquisition of U.S. technology firm Kosmix. The move was likely less about acquiring Kosmix and more about acquiring its founders, Venky Harinarayan and Anand Rajaraman. Ironically, more than a decade earlier, this same duo helped Amazon build its price comparison engine, a bold technology that would come to symbolize Amazon's transparent approach to price and set a new operating standard in online retail. Amazon's CEO, Jeff Bezos, eventually bought their company Junglee for $250 million. One can only speculate how Bezos must have felt seeing that twelve years later, Harinarayan and Rajaraman would become the linchpins in an effort to reclaim the very ground the two had helped Amazon win from Walmart.

By all accounts, though, what the Kosmix team discovered when it lifted the hood on Walmart was daunting. According to those close to the project, the company had been running a rat's nest of off-the-shelf solutions, disparate, disconnected systems and antiquated platforms. For the next year, Kosmix, which was subsequently renamed @WalmartLabs, dedicated itself to completely overhauling the retail battleship.

Initially the results appeared to pay off. In the fourth quarter of 2013, Walmart reported a 30 percent increase in its ecommerce sales. Regrettably for Walmart, however, those initial gains steadily evaporated over ensuing years. As of its first quarter 2016 earnings report, Walmart's ecommerce business increased only 7 percent, which meant it not only trailed the pace of ecommerce growth at Amazon, but also the retail industry as a whole.

In 2016, Walmart CEO Doug McMillon, in a show of just how serious Walmart was about growing its digital business, conditioned shareholders to expect softened profitability to support a $2 billion investment in future technology. Wall Street punished the retailer with the largest drop in its stock value in seventeen years, highlighting a peculiar inequity: when Amazon burns profit to invest in the future, it's called visionary; when Walmart does it, it's called a disaster.

Undeterred, in June of 2016 Walmart entered an alliance with JD.com, China's second-largest business-to-consumer ecommerce company. It was another in a series of efforts to extract a share of the burgeoning Chinese market, something that had previously proven challenging for Walmart. The JD.com deal was aimed at leveraging Walmart's war chest of capital while tapping JD's deep cultural and market knowledge. The deal would prove to be only a warm-up for what came next.

On August 8, 2016, Walmart announced the largest single startup acquisition in history with its reported intent to purchase Jet.com, a one-year-old, U.S.-based ecommerce player, for $3 billion. Jet was founded by Mark Lore, who previously had founded Quidsi, another startup acquired by Amazon in 2010. After leaving Amazon in 2013, Lore went on to found Jet with a simple operating thesis. Lore believed that by deploying advanced analytic technology, Jet could out-price Amazon, and in doing so, carve out a sustainable number two position in the market—a thesis Walmart clearly bought into. Jet not only brought a unique pricing model and access to better online product selection, it also brought Lore, who agreed to remain at the helm of Jet.

In my opinion, however, the Jet deal seemed an attempt to address one of Walmart's deepest and most significant obstacles to online growth: its own customers. Generally speaking,

Walmart's customer base tended not to line up well with the profile of the online power-shopper. As one analyst put it, "Its core customer isn't the most wired or tech savvy shopper out there."[3] Ironically, the very customer that once paved Walmart's unprecedented path to retail domination had become one of its greatest existential threats. Without younger, more urban and higher-income consumers who indexed well to shopping online, Walmart's fortunes were unlikely to turn. Jet.com, with its focus on precisely those consumer segments, could potentially provide the much-needed injection of youthful customers that Walmart needed. The jury is still out on whether Jet.com will be the antidote Walmart so desperately needs or go down in history as a $3 billion bauble. Moreover, with a growing cast of ex-Amazoners among its ranks, one can't help but wonder if Walmart's strategy is simply to become Amazon.

But to characterize this as a battle waged solely between Amazon and Walmart would be misleading. Just about every major retailer in North America and Europe is feeling the effects of Amazon. In the U.S., for example, Amazon's share of the ecommerce marketplace today is greater than that of Walmart, Apple, Macy's, Home Depot, Best Buy, Costco, Nordstrom, Gap Inc., Target, Williams-Sonoma, Kohl's and Sears Holdings combined![4]

As Walmart was to retail, Amazon has become to ecommerce.

Making Amazon even deadlier was the degree to which industry competitors insisted on underestimating the existential threat it posed.

Know
Thy Enemy

AT AN INVESTOR conference in March of 2016, Macy's CEO Terry Lundgren stated that while Amazon may pose some threat in apparel sales, it was likely ill prepared to deal with the harsh realities of online apparel logistics. "They're going to have an interesting challenge when they start getting all those returns coming back online," he told investors, pointing to Macy's experience with online returns as evidence to support his point. Lundgren was making his remarks in response to a recently published research report predicting that Amazon would likely surpass Macy's as America's top apparel seller by 2017.

Around the same time that Lundgren was making these comments, Amazon had a very different focus. It turns out that CEO Jeff Bezos was holding a covert, by-invitation-only conference on robotics, artificial intelligence and space exploration with some of the world's leading experts in each field. While the exact details of what was discussed at the conference remain largely unknown, it's safe to assume that those gathered weren't hashing out how best to clear out last season's ladies' wear collection. In fact, the closest thing to a fashion statement occurred when Bezos arrived wearing a robot costume!

So while Lundgren was ruminating about the intricacies of inventory management and store operations, Bezos was discussing commercialized space flight, cyborgs and cognitive computing. This stark contrast between the headspaces of Amazon and its industry rivals highlights precisely why using conventional retail calculus to strategize against Amazon has proved largely fruitless. As Bezos once said, "Invention requires a long-term willingness to be misunderstood," and misunderstanding Amazon is something its competitors seem perpetually prone to doing. Amazon doesn't think or behave like a retailer at all—something that has won it both kudos and criticism from analysts and investors alike.

One investor complaint has been its historical dearth of profitability. In fact, the most profitable arm of the company is not the retail business at all but the much smaller Amazon Web Services (AWS). The unit began as a computing platform to serve Amazon's internal needs but grew into an outsourced data storage and management service for other organizations. Among its customers are heavy hitters like Netflix, Airbnb and the National Aeronautics and Space Administration (NASA). From a profitability standpoint, AWS is a business that punches way beyond its weight. In fact, a titanic 56 percent of Amazon's total operating income comes from AWS, despite sales in the division amounting to less than 9 percent of the company's total revenue.[1]

However, while this issue of profitability in its retail business has caused periodic pressure from shareholders, Bezos has consistently demonstrated a Houdini-like ability to escape Wall Street's straightjacket. Just when the market appears to be counting Amazon out, it manages to pull off a massive increase in sales, a spike in profitability or a remarkable customer acquisition strategy. That said, Bezos has also steadfastly refused to bow to short-termism in his strategy. Profit, according to Bezos, is a tap that he can turn on anytime he wishes. This is an assertion that shareholders have remained largely content with, perhaps because the company that Bezos founded in 1994 is now a $107 billion[2] per year behemoth, serving 300 million customers worldwide and posting annual sales growth figures that defy gravity.

For example, in the first quarter of 2016 Amazon grew its topline sales by an inconceivable 28 percent, a figure most retail CEOs would ransom their entire families to deliver. What's even more incredible is that of each incremental dollar spent online in the United States, Amazon alone now captures sixty cents![3] Think about that for a moment. Six-tenths of every new dollar spent online is going directly to one company. If that's not a sufficient show of dominance, consider this: for each incremental dollar spent in the North American retail market as a whole, Amazon takes nearly a quarter, leaving the rest of the industry to fight over the remnants.

Prime numbers

The vital organ beating at the center of Amazon is Prime, a subscription program that provides members with free two-day shipping and access to a host of other programs and services for an annual fee of ninety-nine dollars. Prime has somewhat confounded Amazon's competitors because it's not a typical transactional points, credit or discount scheme like those offered by most retailers. Not only does it deliver such benefits as fast, free shipping but, more importantly, it acts as a golden key to the entire Amazon kingdom, which includes digital content and entertainment, media storage, private label products, early access to new e-books and a growing list of Prime-specific offers. I've often said that Prime is like the gateway drug to the heroin that is Amazon. And best of all for Amazon, that drug gets charged to each member's credit card once a year, giving Amazon a recurring and expanding revenue stream.

As it turns out, Prime members are not only more engaged customers, they're also fundamentally better customers. A 2015 report from Consumer Intelligence Research Partners indicates that while Amazon's non-Prime customers spend an average of $625 per year, the average Prime member spends a whopping $1,500! In addition, Prime renewal rates are astonishingly high. In fact, almost 75 percent of thirty-day trial memberships end up renewing for a full year, and 96 percent of second-year paid subscribers renew for a third year.[4] It's no wonder that Amazon works to recruit new Prime members at every turn.

One tool in that effort is Prime Day, a twenty-four-hour exclusive promotion for members featuring a cross-section of items that Amazon offers at deeper-than-usual discounts. With its inaugural start in 2015, Prime Day has, in a mere two years, become the fourth-largest U.S. online shopping day. In 2017 it is widely expected to exceed Black Friday.[5]

Thus, Amazon Prime is not a loyalty program so much as it is a distinct product and service ecosystem underpinned with an elevated customer experience. And with an estimated 54 million people in its subscriber base, it's a tremendously daunting battle-axe that Amazon wields against its rivals across a variety of product and service categories. As if to prove the point, in 2016 the company partnered with Hyundai, delivering Hyundai vehicles directly to the door of Prime members who wished to take them for a test drive. While this promotion was more a marketing stunt than anything else, Amazon was clearly demonstrating that Prime members are a lucrative audience that outside brands are willing to spend extraordinary sums of money to reach.

Spinning the Amazon web

The reality is that while Amazon may be one of the world's most successful online stores, it really isn't a *retailer* in the conventional sense—a fact that makes it infinitely more dangerous to competitors. Instead, it places bets across the board on new technologies, business models, products and services. In fact, from a competitive standpoint, retailers would be wiser to think of Amazon not as a retailer at all but as a data, technology and innovation company that also happens to sell things. Consider that in the past two years alone the company has launched an array of products, programs and platforms, none of which you'd expect to see coming from a traditional "retail" company. These include:

→ **Amazon Art:** online marketplace for limited-edition and original art via select galleries
→ **Echo digital assistant:** artificial intelligence interface built on its Alexa voice technology platform
→ **Flex:** on-demand parcel delivery network
→ **Home Services:** access to plumbing, electrical and other home services
→ **Prime Music:** music streaming service
→ **Prime Pantry:** flat-fee delivery of home goods and nonperishable groceries
→ **Prime Video:** on-demand video service
→ **Smile:** charitable donations
→ **Studios:** original television and movie content creation
→ *Style Code Live:* live fashion shopping show similar to QVC
→ **Supply:** industrial and scientific components
→ **Video Direct:** video network for content creators, akin to YouTube
→ **Wireless:** cellular phones and service plans

Like a black widow spider, Amazon has been spinning a web of innovation, creating a very sticky and effective consumer value ecosystem. For example, by creating great original entertainment content as bait, Amazon brings more people into Prime and thus more sales into its ecommerce business. As Bezos once said, "When we win a Golden Globe, it helps us sell more shoes. And it does that in a very direct way."⁶

What's particularly fascinating about many of Amazon's innovations is that, as with Amazon Web Services, the company doesn't merely think in terms of short-term products and services like most retailers. It thinks in platforms and networks. What I mean is that all of its innovations are built with surplus potential, allowing Amazon to serve businesses outside its walled garden. For example, when it built its Echo device, it released the application programming interface (API) to developers so they could build the technology into their own products. Similarly, if Amazon is able to build a best-in-class shipping network for its own parcels, there's little to prevent it from opening that service up to other companies. Or if its *Style Code Live* show is a hit, there's no reason that it couldn't become a paid marketing platform for products outside Amazon's assortment. In other words, every innovation that Amazon brings to the market becomes yet another strand of sticky silk in that web of value, not only for consumers but for other businesses as well.

This ability to innovate on a different strategic plane makes anticipating Amazon's next move difficult and leaves many of its competitors relegated to follower status. Its capacity to run so many parallel experiments across its business is unprecedented. Moreover, its high threshold for failure within the innovation process is unusual and something the company wears like a badge of honor. "Amazon," Bezos has said, "is the best place to fail." Failure is something Bezos and his team appear more than willing to risk, if it means putting his competitors out of business.

So, what Terry Lundgren and many of his retail colleagues might see as the unyielding constraints and inescapable realities of operating a retail company, Amazon sees as nothing more than archaic speed bumps on the highway to becoming the main artery for everything in a consumer's life. Rather than adhering helplessly to the anachronistic rules of a centuries-old industry, Amazon instead appears more intent on reinventing the industry itself.

And with respect to Lundgren's prognostication about Amazon's likely hurdles, it's precisely these sorts of dismissals and mischaracterizations of Amazon that pump it with the oxygen it needs to grow. It's worth noting that in June of 2016 Lundgren stepped out of his role as the CEO of Macy's in the face of declining sales, and one month later, Bezos became the third-richest man on Earth. Karma's a bitch.

Yet, as remarkable as Amazon is, it's only the most notable actor in an exponential global ecommerce growth story.

A One-Click
World

IN 2015, GLOBAL ecommerce grew to $1.592 trillion. If that number—1.592 trillion—doesn't wow you, what should give you pause is that it represents a 21 percent[1] year-on-year increase—a staggering rate of growth, especially when contrasted to the average 6 or so percent growth for the global retail industry as a whole during the same time period.

Despite its maturity, the U.S. online commerce market grew a dizzying 14.6 percent in 2015,[2] reaching almost $342 billion. In fact, since 2005, there have been only two years—2008 and 2009, the brink of the global recession—in which U.S. ecommerce multiples receded below double-digit levels. Meanwhile, year-on-year U.S. retail growth as a whole, dating back as far as 1992, has never exceeded 9 percent.[3] Never.

And as for the struggle between online and brick and mortar, U.S. consumers are clearly voting with their clicks. More than two-thirds of Americans shop online monthly, with 33 percent in 2015 shopping online weekly—up 9 percent from the year prior.[4] It's clear to anyone watching that America remains a hot-bed of ecommerce growth.

But the U.S. market is merely the antipasto before the all-you-can-eat buffet that is China. In 2015, China surpassed the United States to become the world's largest ecommerce market, with sales of close to $600 billion. Between 2014 and 2015, Chinese ecommerce grew at a flabbergasting rate of 33 percent. In fact, by 2015 China had twice as many Internet users as the U.S. had people, and 89 percent of those users could access the Internet on a mobile device. And get this; only roughly 50 percent of China's total population today is even connected to the Internet! One can only imagine what sorts of numbers China's online economy will throw off when it reaches near-full connectivity.

The beast from the east

On November 11, 2016, as the sun rose in Asia and most of the Western world slept, something truly astonishing happened.

Every November 11, Chinese consumers celebrate what has come to be known as Singles Day, which refers to the fact that the date November 11 can also be expressed as 11/11 or four singles. Originating in 1993, Singles Day began as a day for young, unattached people to get together for parties, blind dates or other social events. As the celebration grew in popularity, it caught the eye of opportunistic retailers, who used the occasion to target consumers (single or otherwise) with promotions. Leading the charge was ecommerce giant Alibaba.

Alibaba is the creation of Jack Ma, a Chinese entrepreneur. Born Ma-Yun, he was raised in the capital city of Hangzhou, China. He learned English as a child by offering free city tours to English-speaking visitors in exchange for their tutelage. Success, however, was hardly a straight line for Ma, who after two failed attempts at his university entrance exams, was finally accepted to the Hangzhou Teachers College. Upon graduation, though, he applied to and was rejected by a string of companies, including KFC. Eventually he secured work teaching English and went on to start his own translation business while working part-time to make ends meet.

One day in 1995, while on a trip to the U.S., a friend showed Ma the Internet, which he, like many living in China, had not yet been exposed to. That experience would prove to inexorably alter the future of global retail for decades to come. It was in that moment, after performing a purely random search for Chinese-branded products which happened to return no search results, that Ma recognized the degree to which Chinese businesses lacked representation on the Internet and was inspired to begin his own China-based startup. He created, as he put it, a "Chinese Yellow Pages," investing the humble sum of seven thousand Yuan, or about fourteen hundred dollars, of his own money. After a year of work, and a degree of success, Ma ended up accepting the equivalent of $185,000 from China Telecom in a merger that would eventually see him lose control over the company and resign.

However, the genie, as they say, was out of the bottle by then. The potential of the Internet and Ma's own entrepreneurial drive proved an infectious combination, and in 1999, he persuaded seventeen of his friends to invest in a new venture. The group cobbled together the equivalent of sixty thousand dollars to start the company that would come to be known as Alibaba. As it turned out, it was sixty thousand dollars well spent. In 2016, Alibaba's market capitalization sat at slightly more than $200 billion dollars and Jack Ma, the once awkward kid who failed his entrance exams and was believed unworthy of a job with KFC, now sits atop one of the largest retail empires on Earth.

But I digress . . . back to Singles Day!

On November 11, 2016, in the very first hour of Singles Day, Alibaba sold an astounding US$5 billion worth of merchandise. You read that correctly—$5 billion (with a B) in sales in sixty minutes. Frankly, it was a tough figure for me to wrap my head around. For perspective, consider that this sales figure equates to approximately $83 million in sales per minute or $1.4 million per second. Put a different way, the average Home Depot store sells approximately $36 million in goods annually. So, in each of the first 60 *minutes* of Singles Day, Alibaba was transacting significantly more than what two—count 'em, two—Home Depot big-box stores sell in a full fiscal *year*. If that still isn't hitting home, consider that the first hour of Alibaba's sales that day almost doubled the combined online sales of every retailer in America on Black Friday.

Alibaba finished up Singles Day 2016 selling more than $20 billion worth of merchandise—a one-day sales figure that more than doubles eBay's 2015 full-year revenue![5] Moreover, for Alibaba it represented a sales surge of more than 40 percent from only one year prior.[6]

For anyone who earns their living in the retail industry, this was a nothing short of a seismic event in ecommerce and a historic juncture from which all sense of the scale and proportion of online retail would change forever. Alibaba achieved a feat that dumbfounded even the most battle-hardened ecommerce observers and Internet evangelists. On November 11, 2016, the beast from the east roared, and in doing so, shifted the axis of online retail forever.

> "You should learn from your competitor, but never copy. Copy and you die." JACK MA

Alibaba is so large that several eBays could fit comfortably in its financial shadow. In 2015, the company sold an astonishing

$476 billion worth of merchandise across its ecommerce plat-forms.[7] More remarkable still is that while most ecommerce companies are criticized for being top-line heavy but bot-tom-line bare, Alibaba routinely generates gross profit mar-gins in the 30 percent range, consistently delivering more bottom-line profit than Amazon and eBay combined!

Yet, while growth in the Chinese ecommerce market has captured much of the global spotlight, it would be impossible to properly calibrate the overall potential scale of global ecom-merce without discussing India.

Betting on Bharat

Although ecommerce in India today stands at a comparatively tiny US$16 billion, Morgan Stanley estimates that within four short years, that figure may balloon by seven times—a number that's being fueled by exponential growth in connectedness. For example, in the time it takes you to read this sentence, almost twenty Indians will connect to the Internet for the first time, a rate of three new users per second. Ecommerce is also projected to single-handedly create as many as 12 million new jobs in India through 2025.[8]

In 2016, India surpassed the U.S. as the second-most Internet-connected global market, and with Internet usage growing at approximately 40 percent per year,[9] it's estimated that by 2030 more than a billion Indians will be online. Indian mobile adop-tion is also growing at a staggering pace. In 2016, one in four mobile devices was a smartphone, a figure that sat at only one in six a year before.

And in more good news for brands, India not only happens to be the world's fastest-growing economy, it also offers phe-nomenally good demographics, housing the world's largest population of millennials. In fact, the median age in India is an astonishing twenty-seven years old, compared to thirty-eight in the United States, forty-one in the United Kingdom and forty-two in Canada.[10] So I ask you, if you're Nike, where would you rather sell running shoes?

In an effort to unlock India's obvious treasure, companies such as Alibaba, Amazon and others have invested heavily in a range of startups. From short-term loan programs for small merchants and payment protection for consumers to intricate plans and alliances to streamline supply chains, these online leviathans are betting big on India.

Those bets, it seems, are paying off. Between 2014 and 2015, the top three ecommerce sites in India, Flipkart, Amazon and Snapdeal, posted sales greater than India's top ten offline retailers.[11] In fact, it's believed by many that it may only be a few years before online commerce surpasses total offline commerce in India—an unprecedented feat in any market.

Retail disruption

For a long time, retailers remained dismissive of the threat that pure-play ecommerce companies posed. Executives were quick to point to the fact that, despite the growth of ecommerce, the majority of retail sales happened within the walls of a physical store—a figure that is dropping at a precipitous pace.

By 2013, however, it had become apparent to most that the velocity and scale of ecommerce were far from abating. Indeed, the rampant growth of ecommerce had become an inescapable fact. Moreover, companies such as Alibaba were not only posting monstrous sales gains and customer acquisition numbers, they were now also delivering profits, overcoming what had long been cited as a fatal shortcoming of ecommerce companies. By the fiscal year ending March 2013, Alibaba posted US$1.6 billion net profit, representing an astonishing 28.6 percent of revenue![12] While Amazon wasn't yet profitable at the time, it was nonetheless posting sales approaching $68 billion and increasing at the blinding pace of more than 20 percent each year.

There was a time when retailers could feel secure in the belief that buying certain categories of goods, such as clothing, furniture and automobiles, online was problematic. Increasingly, however, there are no safe-haven categories. In fact, Alibaba recently set a Guinness world record, selling sixty-five hundred automobiles online in one day! So yes, if you're a car dealer, you can get nervous now.

The fact is, if this were only about Amazon and Alibaba, it might not change the situation the retail industry finds itself in, though it would at least be easier to pinpoint potential disruption in the market. Behind Amazon and Alibaba, however, is an ever-replenishing hoard of startups that are pushing the level of chaos to a fevered pitch and almost constantly blindsiding retail category incumbents.

In 2016, for example, Unilever paid an astonishing $1 billion for startup men's subscription retailer Dollar Shave Club, a brand that began just four years earlier. With 3 million subscribing customers and $200 million in sales, Dollar Shave Club is now giving established brands such as Gillette a run for their money.

Also founded in 2012, Blue Apron has quickly accelerated with its offering of delivered ingredients for home-cooked meals. Valued at $2 billion, the company is now selling 3 million meals per month and giving grocery incumbents shit fits in the process. Even being Costco isn't safe anymore. Boxed Wholesale, founded in 2013, lets online shoppers buy in bulk at wholesale prices without ever setting foot in a Costco or any other club store. The company has raised more than $136 million in capital and has hired hundreds of employees since its launch.

As I write this, a staggering 5,721 startups are listed on one angel investment website alone (Angel List). There are no longer any categories of service or merchandise that are safe havens from digital disruption. If an online alternative to what you retail hasn't been created, I can almost assure you that someone is working on it.

So, if you're a retailer, the mathematical reality of the situation should be sinking in. If overall global ecommerce continues to grow each year by double-digits while brick and mortar plods along in the low singles, somebody ceases to exist.

The Delivery
Arms Race

THE REAL CHALLENGE for ecommerce companies is no longer to convince consumers to buy online, but rather to get the millions upon millions of items we're buying to us in an ever-shrinking window of time.

In a remarkably short period, our expectations regarding order delivery have risen dramatically. It really wasn't that long ago that if you ordered something online, you were happy to receive it ... *ever*! That might sound like an exaggeration but it's not. It was fairly common for orders to be shipped late, broken, incomplete or to the wrong address. If you ordered something from China and it got to you successfully, you were nothing short of amazed! Today, if something from China can't be on our doorstep in a few days, we're likely to be annoyed. It hardly matters what the item is or where it originates, we want it fast.

This growing need for instant gratification has spawned an army of startups and initiatives aimed at rapid local delivery.

→ Postmates, which began in 2011, now delivers a range of goods, including food and consumer products, in twenty-six U.S. cities.

→ Deliv, founded in 2012, is a crowd-sourced delivery service used by retailers such as Williams-Sonoma and a growing number of malls owned by such companies as General Growth Properties, Westfield and Simon Property Group.

→ Ridesharing service Uber entered the delivery market with UberEATS in 2014, and in October of 2015 it launched a new service called UberRUSH aimed at small businesses that need to ship quickly to local customers. Each delivery costs between five and seven dollars.

→ Amsterdam-based startup TringTring uses an on-demand fleet of bicycle riders to deliver parcels and orders locally.

→ Deliveroo is a U.K.-based startup delivering online orders from more than 750 restaurants in twelve countries.

→ In 2014, Skype co-creators Ahti Heinla and Janus Friis launched Starship Technologies, which developed a terrestrial robot capable of navigating city streets delivering parcels and packages day and night. The small six-wheeled, electrically powered vehicle can travel autonomously for up to three miles, carrying a load about the size of two bags of groceries.

→ Domino's Pizza in New Zealand has developed and tested an autonomous delivery vehicle that both warms pizzas and cools beverages.

→ Instacart, now valued at more than $2 billion, is one of a rising tide of grocery delivery startups. In all, nearly forty companies now use on-demand shoppers to pick and deliver grocery and fast-food orders in the U.S. and other countries.[1]

The robots are coming

As you might expect, one of the highest-profile instigators in this delivery arms race has been Amazon. In 2013, in what many initially thought was a promotional stunt, Amazon announced

The Starship Technologies delivery robot.
IMAGE COURTESY OF STARSHIP TECHNOLOGIES

its intention to test airborne parcel delivery with the use of remotely piloted drone quadcopters. As it turned out, the company couldn't have been more serious. In a series of promotional videos, Amazon demonstrated that its intention was to reduce the fulfillment time on orders from days to hours, perhaps even minutes.

Many felt Bezos had lost it. The idea of thousands of drones hurtling through the sky delivering parcels seemed almost laughable to most. What few people knew, however, was that companies such as DHL were already routinely using drones to deliver pharmaceuticals to remote regions of Germany. Bezos wasn't dreaming up drone delivery. It was already happening. Moreover, the notion that Amazon would go to such lengths to deliver quickly actually fit perfectly within the company's strategic narrative. From the beginning, Bezos has made it clear that, while Amazon would always attempt to remain competitive on item pricing, it would ultimately win on the breadth of its selection and the unparalleled convenience of its shopping experience. Airborne delivery was a clear shot across the bow of the retail industry, signifying just how far Amazon was prepared to go to dominate on last-mile delivery to consumers.

In 2016, after much perseverance, the company began a series of approved tests in the U.K. that involved flying drones beyond the line of sight of the operator—a request that has so far been rejected by the U.S. Federal Aviation Administration. But while the futuristic nature of drone delivery has certainly dominated headlines, Amazon has been quietly stitching together the pieces of what appears to be a far more practical and game-changing delivery infrastructure.

For example, in 2012 the company purchased Kiva Systems Inc. for $775 million. The company makes robots equipped to move items efficiently through tight warehouse spaces. At the time, Amazon was battling ballooning headcounts in its warehouses: between 2010 and 2011 alone, they rose by 67 percent.[2] Kiva robots seemed the perfect means of increasing productivity while stemming labor costs.

Today more than thirty thousand Kiva robots operate in thirteen Amazon fulfillment centers, each of which can hold 50 percent more inventory than non-Kiva warehouses.[3] The net result, according to Amazon, has been a 20 percent decrease in its operating costs and a reduction in the average pick-to-ship cycle from sixty or seventy minutes to fifteen minutes.[4] A note from Deutsche Bank estimates that if Amazon were to bring Kiva technology to its remaining fulfillment centers, the result would be an additional $2.5 billion in operating cost reductions. Not too shabby for a $775 million investment.

In 2014, the company raised the delivery stakes considerably by adding an additional perk—Prime Now—to its Prime membership program. Prime Now offered existing members free two-hour shipping on a range of products within select major global markets such as Paris, Berlin, Manhattan and London.

Also in 2014, Amazon blew industry minds when it applied for a patent for what it called "anticipatory shipping," a proposed system to ship products to customers before they ordered them, perhaps even before they realized they wanted them! The patent suggested that Amazon would be able to use predictive analytics to anticipate what a particular customer might order, based on prior order history. On the surface of it, it seems like a crazy notion. However, if one imagines a world where AmazonFresh grocery delivery trucks are visiting homes once, twice or more times each week, Amazon's ability to predict household needs, preferences and ordering frequency becomes very real indeed. Once its data store on a given customer is robust enough, Amazon will know what that customer is likely to order before they know it themselves.

It doesn't end there. By late 2015, Amazon launched a "last-mile" delivery pilot program, taking a page from the strategies of such disruptors as Postmates. The program, dubbed Amazon Flex, allowed anyone twenty-one or older with a vehicle, a clean driving record and an Android smartphone to earn extra cash delivering for Amazon. Beginning in cities where the two-hour Prime Now delivery option was in operation, the company agreed to pay successful applicants between eighteen and twenty-five dollars per hour, with shifts lasting anywhere between two and twelve hours. Not only was Amazon building the infrastructure required for delivery dominance, it was scaling its own flexible, on-demand workforce to cover the crucial last mile of delivery!

Fulfilling ambition

Part of Amazon's willingness to invest in shipping stems from the fact that in addition to being one of the planet's largest online sellers, it has also become one of its largest third-party logistics providers through a little-known unit called Fulfillment

One of Amazon's dedicated 767F cargo aircraft.

by Amazon. For a fee, Amazon picks, packs and ships products directly to consumers for its pool of more than 2 million third-party merchants. In the long run, the Fulfillment by Amazon service saves merchants money but it also significantly subsidizes Amazon's own overall handling and shipping infrastructure costs.

It's my belief that Amazon's ambitions go far beyond merely finding ways to move its own products more efficiently. In fact, I believe we're witnessing Amazon's construction of a delivery empire to rival those of companies such as United Parcel Service (UPS) and FedEx. For example, in November of 2015, largely in response to a holiday shipping snafu that Amazon attributed to failures on the part of UPS, the company entered into what it said was a deal to buy "thousands" of semitrailers to more effectively move inventory from its warehouses to its fulfillment centers. In addition, the company filed a patent proposing that these trucks also be used as mobile distribution centers that can locate as necessary based on seasonal activity, sales flow and even time of day.

Kicking it up a notch, Amazon struck a deal with Air Transport Services Group (ATSG) in March of 2016, whereby ATSG will operate an air transport fleet of twenty 767F cargo planes to support one- and two-day delivery. In addition to operational service, the deal gives Amazon warrants to buy just shy of 20 percent of ATSG over the five years following the deal.

A month later, rumors erupted that Amazon may have been in negotiations to purchase Frankfurt-Hahn Airport in Germany. The airport, which had been losing money for some time, had been for sale since February of the same year. Amazon, according to a German newspaper, was one of three bidders to come forward.

It's precisely this long view of strategy that makes Amazon so troublesome. While most retailers are struggling to play checkers, Amazon has become a grand master of chess, always thinking several moves ahead in an effort to checkmate unwitting retailers. As analyst Scott Galloway put it, "The strategy of Amazon is the last mile strategy or last man standing. A multi-billion-dollar investment, and reaching the last mile through incredible fulfillment infrastructure, hoping that other retailers have to follow them and that those other retailers run out of oxygen because no other retailer has access to the same cheap capital."[5] And he's right. Retailers of all sizes are scrambling to keep pace with the delivery standards that Amazon is now making table stakes.

→ Nordstrom recently acquired Dsco, a company that provides cloud services to improve supply chain fulfillment on ecommerce orders.

→ Walmart has entered into experiments with ridesharing services Lyft and Uber to get orders from stores to customers.

→ Target has made high-profile executive hires from both Amazon and Apple to redesign its delivery structures.

→ U.K. grocer Sainsbury's opened its first "dark store" in 2016. The 185,000-square-foot store and up to nine hundred staff will enable same-day delivery to more than thirty local markets.

→ Canada's Hudson's Bay Company recently invested more than $60 million in a new and almost entirely automated distribution facility.

By so completely shifting shoppers' expectations for fast and free shipping, Amazon has now rewritten the rules, forcing the retail industry as a whole to play by them or die. And many are dying. Retailers across the globe are struggling against this rising flood of online sales. Many more are downsizing, some are closing stores, others are consolidating and an alarming number are defaulting on loans. Some are flatly declaring bankruptcy.

A short list of the retailers with significant store closures includes:

→ **Abercrombie & Fitch**
→ **Aéropostale**
→ **American Apparel**
→ **American Eagle**
→ **Austin Reed**
→ **Barnes & Noble**
→ **Ben Sherman**
→ **Blacks**
→ **Blue Inc**
→ **Bootlegger**
→ **Brantano Footwear**
→ **British Home Stores (BHS)**
→ **Chapters/Indigo**
→ **Cleo**
→ **Costa Blanca**
→ **Debenhams**

→ Dick Smith

→ Future Shop

→ Gap

→ Grand & Toy

→ Guess

→ HMV

→ Jacob

→ JCPenney

→ Macintosh Retail Group

→ Macy's

→ Mexx

→ My Local

→ Office Depot

→ Parasuco

→ RadioShack

→ Ricki's

→ Sears Holdings

→ Sony

→ Sports Authority

→ Staples

→ Target

→ Tesco

→ Vroom & Dreessmann (V&D)

→ Walgreens

→ Woolworths

Closures on U.K. high streets have been devastating. Net closures in 2014 reached 987, more than triple those from the year before. And, in the U.S., which is estimated to have at least double the retail square footage per capita of any other nation, it's estimated that one-third of all shopping malls will soon fail.

While Amazon may not be the sole culprit in all these closures, its impact on retailers cannot be underestimated. And it's not just retailers that are feeling pressured by Amazon. Collateral damage has affected less likely players in the market too, including the company many of us have come to view as being synonymous with the Internet itself: Google.

Search and Destroy

In 2013, Google launched a trial of what it called Google Shopping Express, a service that allowed shoppers to order from a variety of participating retailers and have their orders delivered the same day within the Silicon Valley and San Francisco markets. The program was later renamed Google Express and expanded to include more cities.

To the analyst community, this move made perfect sense. After all, if shoppers were going to Google to find products and retailers, Google could and should begin to leverage that traffic and intent to buy by offering consumers a more convenient portal for ordering across multiple retailers. Google Express would capture a percentage of the revenue from the sale and at the same time, develop a valuable trove of data on search and purchase behavior that it could offer back to participating retailers. The motivation for Google to enter the shopping arena seemed entirely calculated and logical.

What few knew at the time, however, was that one of the urgent underlying motivations for Google Express was that Google was bleeding search traffic to Amazon. Increasingly, Amazon was not simply the top organic result in a Google search; Amazon was becoming the default search engine itself, with customers bypassing Google entirely when looking for products. One study suggested that up to 55 percent of product-related searches are now being performed on Amazon instead of Google.[6]

So while the rest of the global retail industry navel-gazes and contemplates how to become "omnichannel," it's estimated that by 2019, retail ecommerce sales will hit an estimated $1.671 trillion and make up 7.4 percent of the total retail market worldwide.[7] And even more unnerving, by 2020, Amazon, Alibaba and eBay alone will have secured an estimated 39 percent of the global online retail market.[8]

Marc Andreessen's prophecy—that retailers are going to go out of business and that ecommerce will become the place everyone buys—seems to be standing up to scrutiny. Ecommerce companies definitely seem to be the sharks in the water and retailers the hapless surfers getting picked off one by one. Any retailers still clinging to the hope that the Internet will somehow overlook their category or leave them unscathed are, to put it bluntly, delusional. The only remaining question is, can retailers do anything to stop the feeding frenzy?

Requiem
for Don Draper

MY WORK PUTS me at fifty or so retail industry events in various parts of the world each year, and so I meet a tremendous number of people in the field. What I can tell you is that most of the senior retail executives I encounter are between forty-five and sixty-five years old, and a significant proportion of them are baby boomers born between 1946 and 1964.

It's safe to say, therefore, that the retail industry is largely being led by people who grew up believing in two immutable laws governing business strategy. They were that

→ *Mass media was dependably effective.* As a marketer, you knew how many people in a market took delivery of the daily newspaper. You knew how many people subscribed to a particular magazine or how many people watched *Seinfeld* or any number of TV shows. These were numbers you could take to the bank. Hire a good agency, make nice ads, put them where people would see them and *bingo*—foot traffic to your business! And if consumers didn't answer the call, the only possible explanation was that you didn't buy enough media. We were conditioned to count on mass media.

→ *The consumer's path to purchase was linear and largely predictable.* Consumers moved through a very identifiable series of narrowing steps from brand awareness to the eventual transaction. Furthermore, brands and retailers could control almost all the data inputs along that path, as consumers lived in a veritable vacuum and depended almost solely on the information provided by brands and retailers to guide their decisions. In other words, retailers held the balance of power.

For well over half a century, these have been the understood terms of engagement between retailers and consumers. The *rules*, if you will. Therefore, the reflexive tendency of many conventional retailers is to spend more advertising dollars when times get tough.

In Canada, for example, floundering Sears stores went through six CEOs in three years with an average tenure of six short months. The chain had been precipitously losing share to other retailers and, in particular, getting its lunch eaten online. Unsurprisingly, in an effort to defibrillate the brand, each new CEO mounted a flourish of slick ad campaigns talking about the "big changes" shoppers could expect. However, none of these expensive attempts to market the brand as new and exciting were enough to move the needle even an inch, and ultimately the only big changes were the nameplates on the corner office door.

Which raises the questions:

→ Is advertising the answer to the retail carnage wrought by ecommerce?

→ Can marketing dollars stop the onslaught of companies such as Alibaba, Amazon and the other online heathens battering down the gates?

→ Can well-crafted and cunningly purchased media exposure save the day as it once did?

Media is abundant; attention is scarce

Today we have more advertising than ever. In 2015, for example, advertising spending was $552 billion worldwide, up nearly 4 percent from the year prior. In the U.S., the figure reached $187 billion, of which $79 billion (a full 42 percent) is still being spent on the granddaddy of all media—television.

Despite what you might hear in the press, television as a medium is hardly dead. Americans still watch an amazing 4.3 hours of television per day.[1] Moreover, a recent U.K.-based study suggests that 90 percent of consumers rate television ads as being far and away the most memorable advertising format.[2] The problem is not that we're not watching television; it's that we're not watching *television advertising*. At least not nearly the way we used to.

Much of the problem revolves around a key TV ad metric, *reach*. Reach is simply the number of viewers who *could* see a particular ad. It's this number of potential viewers that advertising executives zero in on when deciding where to place their advertisements.

So is reach still a valid metric? I've explored this question by straw polling audiences when I'm delivering presentations. First I ask for a simple show of hands from those who still watch broadcast television. It's usually most of the audience. Then I ask those who routinely have their laptop, mobile device or tablet with them while watching television to keep their hand raised. Invariably almost everyone keeps their hand up, and I'm sure you may be thinking that you would too. I follow by asking what those with their hand raised typically do when the program they're watching breaks for commercials. As you can appreciate, the responses then vary. Some check their e-mail;

Dual-screen engagement now competes
for consumer viewing attention.
MARCO PIUNTI

others check their Facebook page. Some upload photos to Instagram and others shop online, watch a video or engage in some other distraction. What is absolutely consistent across the board is that almost no one is watching the commercials—not deliberately anyway. And you're probably not either. Why would you? You have a supercomputer filled with fun and entertaining content in the palm of your hand! Why on earth would you watch dull commercials?

And this isn't new behavior. As far back as 2011, a survey conducted by Nielsen discovered that 40 percent of smartphone and tablet owners were splitting their attention between the TV and these other devices while watching a program. While wishful ad executives have argued that consumers may be able to multitask adequately to absorb ambient advertising, studies show that this is likely not the case and that advertisers would be better advised to regard dual-screen viewers as an obstacle.[3]

Spreading our attention across devices is having a devastating impact on the effectiveness of advertising. Going back to our reach metric, we might know how many people are watching *The X Factor* tonight, for example, yet we have no bloody clue how many will be watching the commercials. But if my highly unscientific hands-on polling method is any indication, it isn't many.

Cross-platform consumption

The other reach-killing factor is that consumers are no longer shackled to live broadcasts as the only means of consuming programming. They are now watching television across devices, services, platforms and timeframes. Nonlinear TV programming, as it's called, is completely changing the advertising dynamic.

In fact, Nielsen had to change its rating system to account for it. To understand audience preferences across the broad spectrum of devices and channels on which programming can now be consumed, Nielsen now uses a system it calls "total audience measurement" to count every view across every screen involved in consuming a piece of programming. What it found was stunning. In one early test, a mere 45 percent of the audience was actually watching a client's broadcast drama during its initial airing. The remaining 55 percent watched the program over a longer timespan and on a multitude of devices, including:

→ **32%:** digital video recorder during the first seven days after it aired
→ **2%:** digital video recorder between 8 days and 35 days after it aired
→ **7%:** video on demand from within 35 days
→ **6%:** via a connected TV device
→ **8%:** streaming via PC, mobile device or tablet

And any marketers clinging to the hope that the time-shifting viewer is deliberately watching their commercials may want to rethink that strategy. The same study in the U.K. suggested that 86 percent of viewers who use a digital video recorder (DVR) are practically pounding their clenched fist on the fast-forward button to zoom past commercials.

Even premium entertainment like the Academy Awards and sporting event broadcasts like the Super Bowl that have traditionally been advertising gold are proving to be a road to nowhere. Audience ratings for the 2016 Olympic Games, for example, trailed the 2012 London Games' numbers by 17 percent,[4] clearly reflecting this growing multiscreen universe.

So the disparity between *reach* (the opportunity to consume an advertisement) and *impression* (the consumption of an advertisement) is now gaping and growing rapidly. Moreover, it's a problem that can't be easily solved simply by showing more ads, known as *frequency*. This third metric in what used to be the holy trinity of advertising is, of course, rendered useless if reach is broken. If no one is watching your TV ads to begin with, increasing frequency only guarantees that people will ignore them more often than they already are.

What confounds retail marketers even more is that the very consumers they desire most, young consumers, are watching significantly less television than older cohorts. In fact, according to a range of studies, traditional television viewing by millennials aged eighteen to twenty-four has dropped by 38 percent since 2011. For those twenty-five to thirty-four years old, the drop was smaller but still significant at almost 22 percent.[5]

Digital dreams

This drop-off in the effectiveness of conventional advertising formats has led brands to follow the siren call of digital media. Like a school of fish simultaneously veering off course to evade danger, industries have been rapidly and profoundly redirecting advertising spending.

Global advertising spending rose by 4.6 percent in 2015 over 2014, driven largely by digital advertising spending, which grew at more than three times that pace.[6] Particularly conspicuous was the rise in spending on social advertising, which at $23.68 billion in 2015 represented a 33.5 percent increase from 2014. By the end of 2017, spending on social network ads is expected to reach $35.98 billion, representing 16 percent of all digital ad spending worldwide.[7]

Of course, much of what has propelled marketers to make such moves are the intoxicatingly large user numbers that companies such as Facebook, Twitter, Instagram and a host of other social media networks publicize. Clearly, in the world of social media, size still matters. For example, you don't have to go very deep into Facebook's corporate site before you find these sorts of stats:

→ 1.13 billion daily active users on average for June 2016
→ 1.03 billion mobile daily active users on average for June 2016
→ 1.71 billion monthly active users as of June 30, 2016
→ 1.57 billion mobile monthly active users as of June 30, 2016

Twitter, too, is quick to tout its reach:

→ 310 million monthly active users
→ 83 percent active users on mobile
→ 1 billion unique visits monthly to sites with embedded tweets

And of course, Instagram, which bills itself as a community of more than 500 million people.

These numbers are staggering, and I'll be the first to vouch for the idea that social media can be an effective means of connecting with like-minded individuals and spreading non-promotional content that has perceived value. It *can* work.

In addition, Facebook's ever-increasing ability to track and mine information about its users is enough to make the National Security Agency look like amateurs. Most people aren't aware that Facebook uses ninety-eight unique data points to triangulate the moment-to-moment interests, needs and preferences of each of its users—whether they are logged into Facebook or not! Yes, even if you're not logged into Facebook, bits of code and plug-ins scattered elsewhere around the Internet will continue to trace your activity, with a direct pipeline back to the mother ship: Facebook.

The upshot is that if, for example, you are a single, blue-collar worker who recently moved to London and are a fan of rugby, drive a Kia, eat Indian food and have a mother with a birthday in June, each of these and about ninety other pieces of information will be combined to serve you a very different array of ads than another user with a different assortment of data points.

Some people find this level of intrusiveness disturbing and others see it as the price we pay to avoid mass marketing. What is hard to argue is the degree to which Facebook and other free social networks have completely altered both the definition and machination of targeted marketing.

The flaw with Facebook

In their zeal around social marketing, though, large retailers and brands may be overlooking a glaring flaw in the math. Beneath the colossal stats and user numbers that business media are quick to latch onto lie a few caveats that are central to really understanding the potential return on investment, which very few marketers seem aware of or willing to acknowledge. And that's a problem that makes Mark Ritson, adjunct professor at the Melbourne Business School, apoplectic.

In a brilliant presentation (which you should definitely watch on YouTube), Ritson dissects the social media marketing numbers that, all too often, get glossed over. In one especially profound example, he looks at the social media marketing efforts of Australian retailer Woolworths. He points out that as a brand it has amassed 721,000 Facebook likes, which on the face of it seems like a pretty impressive number. But here's where we need to dig a little deeper into the facts. The 721,000 Facebook fans are all the users who have *ever* liked Woolworths on Facebook. What the number doesn't indicate is *recency*, or how many of those users are truly active or engaged currently. As Ritson points out, when one looks only at the number of active users who have engaged with Woolworths on Facebook within a given week, the number drops to only eighty-five hundred, a mere 1.1 percent of the sexier headline number. But, as Ritson notes, here's the real bummer: while Woolworths was dedicating the efforts of its social media team to reaching eighty-five hundred Facebook users, "the brand had 21 million people visit Woolworths stores." In other words, in the midst of the brand chasing (at great expense) 0.0004 percent of its customer base on Facebook, 21 million live, in-the-flesh, human customers walked into its stores. So why not invest instead in more thoroughly delighting the 21 million?

These kinds of dismal payoffs are hardly limited to Woolworths. Similar results apply to most consumer brands looking for love on Facebook. For Ritson, it comes down to a fundamental failure on the part of brands to recognize that they are "the third wheel" in social media. "It's been mis-sold to you," he says. "Social media is for people. It's not for brands."[8] To his point, if you look at the top hundred user accounts on Twitter, there's not a single retailer or consumer brand to be found. Zero. Rather, it's a "who's who" of media networks and celebrities.

To social marketing zealots, this fact will come as heresy, but it's hardly the first time someone has questioned the net value of social media marketing. Nate Elliott, vice president and principal analyst at Forrester Research, recently had this advice for brands:

> There's no community there. This notion of "build a community on Facebook," I've never seen any brand successfully build a long-term community on Facebook. Maybe around a topic for a week, people come together, but conversations aren't threaded. They're not archived. There's never been a meaningful community there. Even pages that get lots of likes on posts, and comments and shares, there's not a community there. The notion that you build a community on Facebook, and that we call people who manage the pages Community Managers, it's always been a pipe dream. If you want a community, you need to build a community, and that means a branded community on a domain you own.[9]

You may be wondering, though, what about all that amazingly targeted advertising? Surely that delivers results? According to Ritson it may not, and the reason has a lot to do with what passes for a successful advertising "impression" on Facebook. For example, let's assume you produce and run an awesome video ad on Facebook. If a user views only a fraction of an inch of the video viewing area and doesn't even make out its content, Facebook would classify it as a *view* and charge you, the marketer, for it. And it gets worse. In fact, an estimated 85 percent of videos on Facebook play with the sound muted,[10] suggesting that as few as 15 percent of users actually ever hear them— something Facebook is now working to change. But here's the really shitty news: if someone watches as little as three seconds of your video, with the sound turned off, you pay for it as a view. Hopefully it's the best three seconds of someone's life and they happen to read lips, otherwise it's pretty much a waste of your marketing budget.

In late 2016, Facebook itself was forced to admit that its method of calculating the average time users spent watching videos was quite significantly flawed. It turns out that by excluding all videos that get viewed for *fewer* than three seconds, Facebook was giving marketers a dramatically inflated view of the overall effectiveness of video on the site. And that metric has been factoring heavily into the decisions marketers make about where and how to spend their ad dollars.

But even if a consumer did see your ad for more than a few seconds, external website ads have a click-through rate of between 2 and 5 percent. So, if we're being honest, how effective can we really expect Facebook marketing to be?

The difficulty is that if you want to market your business on Facebook, you have little choice but to pay to play. Facebook has been making it progressively more difficult for businesses to reach consumers organically, by systematically suppressing unpaid posts and thereby forcing brands to spend more money to reach the same or smaller audiences of consumers. In essence, Facebook is charging brands more and more each year in order to subsidize the free memberships of users who want to share pictures of puppies and kittens. And they're doing so because an abundance of data suggests that no one is going to Facebook to look at ads. Here are the real reasons we're going to Facebook:

→ **52%:** to find out what friends are doing
→ **42%:** to send messages directly to friends
→ **39%:** to keep in touch
→ **20%:** to post videos
→ **15%:** to see what friends are watching/listening to[11]

If you're looking for the percentage of consumers that go to Facebook to hang with brands and retailers, the number is so small it didn't make the list. And this is not a condition that applies only to Facebook; all social media platforms have experienced the same problem when attempting to monetize their audiences.

Same noise, different channel

These facts have some brands rethinking their approach to Facebook entirely. Procter & Gamble (P&G), for example, backed off its heavy use of targeted ads in 2016, when it discovered that this return on investment was lacking compared with its broader digital approaches. P&G, like other brands, was having trouble reconciling the obvious pervasiveness of this new medium with its ultimate cost-effectiveness.

In my view, Facebook has simply become the ABC, NBC or CBS of its era. Just as TV networks once dominated as our go-to source for information, most of us are now tuning in, as it were, to Facebook, and the cost of maintaining the network and its content is supported through advertising revenue. Is there anything really new here? Well, in fact there is. Today consumers are fighting back. For example, 22 percent of adults in the U.K. and 10 percent of Internet users in the U.S. now use online ad blockers, which are essentially napalm for advertisements.[12] It's a trend that is sparking wars between online advertisers and ad-blocking software companies.

To illustrate just how crazy this game of cat and mouse has become, Facebook announced in August of 2016 that it had devised a workaround that would force ads to show, even when ad-blocking software was being used. On its blog, Facebook told its users that advertising was essential to Facebook's existence; therefore, it was going to jam ads onto users' newsfeeds whether they liked it or not. A mere forty-eight hours later, at least one ad-blocking company had already figured out how to circumvent Facebook's ad-blocker blocker. No doubt this response has set Facebook in motion to create a blocker for the ad-blocker blocker blocker!

My fellow futurist Gerd Leonhard puts it this way: "Every time advertisers build a better mousetrap, they learn the same thing; consumers don't like mousetraps."[13] The elephant in the room here is that advertising doesn't have a channel problem. It has an advertising problem. Consumers just generally hate advertising, and with precious few exceptions, we always have. The difference is that now we have the power and the technology to do something about it.

Brad Jakeman, president of PepsiCo's global beverage group, goes so far as to suggest that the terms "digital marketing" and even "advertising" should go by the wayside. In fact, Jakeman says the entire concept of advertising is based on "polluting" the world with content that people don't want to see. In particular, Jakeman points to his special level of contempt for pre-roll ads—the thirty-second video ads that run before a piece of video content; he feels like they take hours off one's life. At a recent conference he said, "What is even worse is that I know the people who are making it [the pre-roll ad] know that I'm going to hate it. Why do I know that? Because they tell me how long I am going to have to endure it—thirty seconds, twenty seconds, fifteen seconds. You only have to watch this crap for another ten seconds and then you are going to get to the content that you really wanted to see. That is a model of polluting content that is not sustainable."[14]

I'd take Jakeman's theory a step further and suggest that advertising, as a concept, is simply no longer sustainable. We can dress it up, call it different things and deliver it through new channels, but it's still advertising and it's still horrible.

My advice to retailers and brands today is that their going-in assumption needs to be that there is no longer any way to *buy* enough attention to succeed. If you're not good enough at what you do to drive earned media, attention and reputation, then there's no amount of paid advertising that will save you. Your advertising can be content-driven, programmatic, location-based or a good old-fashioned TV commercial—it doesn't matter. The odds of piercing the noise and reaching people, in numbers, who happen to give a shit about your brand are almost nil.

And even if you could push enough messages through the chaos in the market to reach your target consumer, you then face another entirely different challenge. That neat, tidy and linear path to purchase that we talked about earlier is now a convoluted maze of different channels, touch points, platforms and devices. Consumers may begin their journey toward a brand through any number of different means, many of which a brand has little control over. And far from narrowing, as used to be the case, the number of brand and product alternatives actually expands exponentially as the journey continues.

We may, for example, hear about a product for the first time on Facebook or Twitter, not because the brand serves us an ad but simply because a friend happens to mention it. That might take us to the brand's website, where we are directed to a local store. We may visit the store but then return to the web to begin researching alternative products or reading reviews. We may not buy anything until weeks or months later. Ultimately we may return to the original retailer's website, where we download its app but make the purchase online sometime later while sitting in a coffee shop. What marketer could possibly account for this sort of journey, much less control the consumer's experience along its entire path—a path paved with entirely new consumer needs and preferences?

The End
of the Beginning

OUR CONSUMER BRAINS have been completely rewired with new expectations. Our online experiences are shaping our expectations of our offline experiences. We have been reprogrammed, so to speak, which is creating even more challenges for retailers and their marketing teams. As a case in point, I can still recall my first trip to a Best Buy store. I remember being dumbfounded by what seemed, at the time, to be an astonishing inventory of products. In particular, I recall being amazed by the number of televisions on display—about seventy-five, I suppose. It seemed incredible. By comparison, if I visit Amazon today and search the keyword "televisions," more than half a million results come up. *Half a million!* So, in fewer than thirty years, my brain's benchmark for what a great selection of televisions should look like has gone from seventy-five to five hundred thousand.

More importantly, beyond simply offering more to choose from, great ecommerce sites actually make the process of choosing easier. One thousand items on Home Depot's website are infinitely easier to browse, refine, compare and choose from than a hundred of the same products would be in one of Home Depot's cavernous stores.

This fact hit home recently while I was on a shopping trip with my wife to find a faucet for a bathroom we're renovating. We found ourselves in a big-box home improvement store, standing in front of a display of about a hundred different faucets of different sizes, prices, finishes and functionalities. Without saying a word, we both just stood there, glassy-eyed, looking up at the wall of products. After just a short while, we left empty-handed. It wasn't until later that evening that I realized why it was so difficult to decide what to choose. Our brains had become so adapted to online shopping, where one can refine a search, compare items and access loads of well-structured product information, that shopping in a physical store, without the benefit of those tools, had become almost impossible for our brains to manage. The result was essentially a cognitive meltdown.

This growing chasm between the ease and convenience of the online shopping experience versus the challenges and rigors of the offline experience will soon reach a tipping point, and it simply will no longer make sense to venture into the relative information vacuum of a physical store, as we know it today. To remain relevant, retailers will have to imbue their physical environments with the tools, data and technologies that consumers are becoming reliant on to make informed and frictionless decisions.

Mobile mania

Raising the stakes is the fact that this massive new universe of easy-to-shop selection is no longer simply sitting on a laptop in the consumer's home while they're out shopping. It's in their hand, pocket or purse in the form of their mobile device.

Coffee shop patrons glued to their mobile devices.
OKTAY ORTAKCIOGLU

Now, I'm not going to waste ink here trying to convince you that mobile's actually *a thing*. I'm sure you're well aware of that fact already. After all, as far back as 2014, smartphone ownership was already exceeding ownership of feature phones. And, Forrester Research estimates that by 2020 more than 85 percent of all handsets in the world will be smartphones. Furthermore, the smartphone subscriber market will continue to grow at a five-year compounded rate of 9.5 percent through 2020.[1]

Like me, I'm sure you see these statistics playing out around you every day. In every coffee shop, airport, park or other public place, you see people glued to their mobile devices. Go to a concert, an art gallery or on a city tour and you see people experiencing the event through their smartphones. We are literally living our lives through the screens of our devices. For at least 68 percent of us, our mobile device is the first thing we look at in the morning[2]—before checking it another 220 times throughout the average day.[3] One-third of mobile users get anxious at the mere thought of being without their devices. I have to admit that I'm one of them.

I went to dinner alone one night while traveling recently, and no sooner had I sat down than my smartphone battery died. Do you know that sense of panic? It was like my supply of oxygen had been cut off. When the waiter arrived and asked if he could bring me anything, the voice in my head cried out for a phone charger! I restrained myself, but while I waited for the food to arrive, I had to rediscover what one actually does without the benefit of a smartphone.

Whether we like it or not, our lives are increasingly inseparable from our technology, and this reality is having a dramatic impact on how, where, when and even why we buy things. In fact, by the time you're reading this book, at least 50 percent of all retail transactions will involve the web in some way, with an ever-growing percentage of this activity taking place on mobile. The upshot of this digital umbilical cord is that, as consumers, we now expect that anything we want to know, have, see or do is two taps on a piece of glass away.

Facing the future

So with brick-and-mortar retail threatened by ecommerce, and its traditional answer of increasing advertising spending rendered more and more impotent, what does the future hold for the industry? When will the inordinate expansion in online commerce normalize to the growth rate of the retail market as a whole? When will these astronomical year-on-year, double-digit gains in ecommerce ebb back to the earthly rates of say, 3 to 5 percent that the rest of the retail industry is accustomed to? My advice is not to hold your breath. As Winston Churchill famously said, "Now this is not the end. It is not even the beginning of the end. But it is, perhaps, the end of the beginning."[4]

All evidence points to the fact that we are heading into an online retail future that could make ecommerce, as we know it today, look like a Sears, Roebuck & Company Christmas catalog. When we describe to our grandchildren how we used to sit by the light of our computers, clicking on two-dimensional pictures, entering our payment information and then waiting for a petroleum-powered delivery truck to arrive, they will pity us and marvel at how we ever survived.

So what does the future of ecommerce look like? I'll be happy to share what I believe lies ahead, but before we go any further I'm going to give you a choice. As Morpheus from *The Matrix* famously said to Neo, "You have a choice. You take the blue pill, the story ends. You wake up in your bed and believe whatever you want to believe. You take the red pill, you stay in Wonderland and I show you how deep the rabbit hole goes."

In other words, you can close this book now and carry on in your business the way you always have, and no one will be the wiser. You can stick to the beliefs and paradigms that got you to where you are today and hope they carry you through tomorrow. Or you can choose to read on and see where all this might really be going. But if you do, you have to open your mind to what is possible in the future and leave your skepticism here, in the present.

The choice is yours.

MEDIA IS THE STORE

Ecommerce 3.0

I SEE YOU'VE opted for the red pill. Splendid! Let's begin.

The changes taking place in the retail world around us may appear to be binary; that is, as ecommerce grows, brick-and-mortar stores will have no option but to die. And given the plethora of retailers falling by the wayside and the number of stores that are closing, one could easily be led to believe that, as Marc Andreessen has said, "software is eating retail."

At the same time, others are positioning "omnichannel" as the cure-all to retail's problems. They believe that by merging the operational elements of various channels on the back end, consumers will enjoy a "seamless" experience at the front end. Sharing information about customers, products and preferences across channels could breathe new life into a dying business model, and stores, as we know them today, will remain relevant.

The problem with both of these diagnoses is that they're overly simplistic and fundamentally flawed. In fact, what we are witnessing is a historic transition: a trading of places between the conventional roles of media and stores. We are crossing a threshold where media, in all of its forms, is in fact becoming "the store." This sounds awfully Marshall McLuhanesque, I know, but believe me, it's not nearly so heady. The best way for me to explain the transition is with a brief look back at the traditional dynamic that has existed between media and stores.

At the top of the old purchase funnel sat the need to build awareness, an objective achieved largely with the help of advertising media. Typically, advertising had three defined roles: to tell a brand story, to create urgency for a product or service and, above all, to drive consumers down the funnel toward a point of purchase. So if you were a big brand, for example, you dripped your ad with distinct creative and copy, to create a brand impression; you adorned your product with captivating language and imagery, to heighten desire; and, finally, you pointed consumers to places in the market, to buy your product. If a piece of media could effectively do all three of these things, then it was largely viewed as successful and the consumer toddled off to a store to get whatever you were selling.

At the bottom of the funnel sat the purchase, which was traditionally executed at a physical store. The store was responsible for being ready when that piece of advertising hit the market. The store simply waited for customers to beat a path to its door. As long as the store had adequate stock of the advertised item and the staff had a modicum of product knowledge, all they needed to do was to transact the sale. It was simple.

Media was the communication component; the store was the distribution point. And for the better part of three hundred years, this has been the working dynamic between media and stores. But now, in a hyperconnected world, the purchase funnel is being turned upside down and media is becoming the store. There is no longer any friction of distance between the message about the product and the ability of the consumer to buy the product immediately.

Today, I can buy directly from interactive ads in a magazine. I can click on an ad on Facebook and a bot will instantly take my order. I can buy directly from a text message on my smartphone or from a shoppable ad on YouTube. I can buy from a commercial on my smart TV, a video game, a billboard with a quick response (QR) code on it, even a sound or a piece of music. You name it, and I can buy directly from any form of media in the world!

Media is no longer merely a call to action to go to a store, the way it once was. Now, media *is* the store. And because of this new reality, we are entering an entirely new era in ecommerce. Anyone predicting that ecommerce will continue along on a linear and incremental growth path isn't paying attention. Because on the horizon sits an army of technologies and startups poised to propel us into a completely different era of online retail reality. Designers, technologists, mathematicians, software developers, engineers and a new breed of hyperentrepreneurial retailers are training their skill and attention on the retail market. Their goal is to make shopping online infinitely more experiential, intuitive, invisible, instantaneous and even, dare I say, human.

Not only will media even more completely become the store, it will soon become difficult to distinguish the digital from the physical. Media will not only do what stores have traditionally done, but it will do it infinitely better than stores ever have!

We will no longer view ecommerce as something that we *do* but merely something that *is*. It will simply happen all around us all the time, with varying levels of involvement or acknowledgment. Like electricity, we will soon notice ecommerce more by its absence than its presence. Every piece of media, every device, every available surface, including our bodies, will be the store—if we want them to be. Whatever we like will be a whisper away, and much of what we need will come to us without even asking for it.

The store as we've known it will cease to be a physical space, app or website that we make a conscious visit to; it will be with us, around us and even in us (via implantable technology) at all times. Think this all sounds far-fetched? Think again; it's already happening.

The replenishment economy

In 2009, Procter & Gamble began briefing its agencies on what was at the time a completely different and somewhat radical marketing strategy. The company that in many ways had come to define top-down mass marketing was preparing to take an all-new approach to market called *store-back*. Put simply, store-back was centered on the belief that if a marketing idea of any kind couldn't execute effectively at the point of purchase, it simply wasn't worth investing in. Rather than spending copious sums of money broadcasting ad messages to nebulous *consumers*, P&G believed brands were better served to focus keenly on *shoppers* as they took their final steps along the path to purchase.

The shift in strategy was a clear sign to the marketing world that P&G regarded the store shelf—not mass media channels—as the most critical retail battleground and, at the end of the day, the only one that truly mattered. The final few feet of the consumer's journey to a product was, at least in P&G's mind, the ultimate moment of truth. And so rather than marketing campaigns beginning with *the big media play*, P&G adopted the philosophy that all great ideas begin at the shelf and worked back from there.

However, store-back operates on the basis of a flawed assumption: that as we move into the future, we will continue to consciously shop for most items we need on a regular basis.

In fact, a significant percentage of the items we use on a daily, weekly or monthly basis will fade from our consciousness and be ordered for us by our technology. Our homes, autos, appliances, workplaces, pets and even our own bodies will begin to make many of these routine purchase decisions for us. No path to purchase, no influence from marketing along the way and no consideration at the shelf required. It's what I call the *replenishment economy*, a future state in which sensors, devices and robust analytics manage most of our daily, weekly and monthly product needs for us. And it will render today's marketing strategies for consumer packaged goods useless within a decade.

Today it's estimated that some 25 billion connected devices exist on the planet.[1] These include everything from our personal technologies, such as smartphones, tablets, laptops and wearables such as fitness monitors, to the networks of sensors that power city infrastructures, such as traffic lights, electrical grids and closed-circuit cameras.

Some industry insiders, including Cisco Systems chairman John Chambers, believe that over the next decade the number of connected devices on Earth will quite likely explode to 500 billion[2] and include many things we have not yet conceived of. They predict that an array of technologies, including pills and implants that monitor and transmit our vital statistics to health care providers; clothing that measures and anticipates physiological conditions such as dehydration or heart failure; even surfaces in our homes that transform into intelligent and connected portals for communication and commerce, will form a connected blanket of technology over the planet. Places and objects that until now were inanimate, disconnected and "dumb" will have the potential to become intelligent, communicative elements of our lives. All will have the power to speak to us, to one another and to the suppliers they rely on for their needs, and all will be supported by an accelerating cloud computing capability that gives these devices access to an ever-growing ocean of data, intelligence and learning capacity.

Put another way, each and every one of these technologies will become a new *consumer* that can formulate real-time buying decisions based on real-time needs. They will be capable of deciding what items need to be purchased and when, and they will provide advice on where best to buy those products and what price to pay, based on instant, real-time data inputs. These connected devices will constitute a layer of artificial intelligence (AI) that will, in essence, become our external consumer brain. I estimate that a minimum of 25 percent of the consumer decisions we occupy ourselves with today will be entirely relegated to technology by 2025.

I realize that when stated this way, it's a future that sounds strange and distant. In truth, the seeds of this movement have already taken root. Far from being science fiction, the replenishment economy is taking shape today.

The Internet of everything

In 2015, Amazon's introduction of Dash Buttons, simple Wi-Fi-connected devices programmed to order specific products, was a clear step toward this future. Place a Tide Dash Button in your laundry room, for example, and when you need more laundry detergent, you simply push the button. The detergent is then ordered, billed to your Amazon Prime account and shipped. Amazon introduced Dash Buttons for a range of common household products, including Bounty paper towels, Gillette razors and deodorant and Huggies diapers, to name just a few.

"Don't look at the finger… look at where it's pointing."
UNKNOWN

Some people were quick to criticize the setup process for the buttons as being too onerous. Others complained that the product options weren't ideal. Still others felt that the prices were too high. These were valid criticisms. Dash Buttons were hardly perfect. What critics tended to lose sight of, however, was the profound potential for this technology to completely alter the way we shop. Dash Buttons were a bold first attempt on Amazon's part to disrupt and shorten the entire path to purchase.

Amazon understood that the vast majority of our purchases are purely replenishing items that we'd rather not have to remember to buy or drag home from the store. If Amazon could get straight to the shelf in the consumer's home and make it easy to fill that shelf when it was empty, it also understood that it could negate the influence of all competitive marketing. It could essentially shut the door on its competitors.

At it turned out, Dash Buttons were the very first chess move in a much larger ideological platform called Dash Replenishment Service (DRS). This ambitious technology allows for sensors to be built directly into products themselves in order to trigger replenishment orders without any user intervention whatsoever! In introducing the platform, Amazon debuted a Brita water pitcher capable of reordering its own replacement filter cartridges. The Wi-Fi–enabled water container sells for roughly double the cost of a regular Brita. Since then, the company has expanded its DRS-enabled appliances and products to include Brother ink cartridges, Whirlpool and General Electric (GE) washers and dryers and the Gmate SMART blood-glucose monitor. Samsung has also committed to incorporating DRS into a number of its products.

If this isn't enough to scare the hell out of retailers, Amazon has raised the stakes by making DRS an open application, giving *any* companies with listings on Amazon access to the

DRS functionality and allowing them to tinker and build Dash replenishment technology directly into their products.

So, just for a moment, picture a grocery store. Picture the center aisles of that grocery store and imagine the sheer number of products that the replenishment economy will swallow up: detergent, diapers, dog food, personal care products, cleaning products, milk, you name it. In a world with DRS, Amazon could potentially become the default provider for entire aisles of the average grocery store, without the consumer ever having to consciously purchase any of the items.

Now picture a home improvement warehouse store filled with lightbulbs, furnace filters, shingles, swimming pool chemicals. These are just a few of the thousands of home items that will become connected and begin to reorder themselves. Imagine DRS-enabled running shoes, bicycle tires, tennis balls, all of which reorder themselves once they reach a threshold of measured use. Soon, thousands of products will be connected and able to order their own replacements. And beyond Amazon's DRS platform, manufacturers across all categories will undoubtedly start to build Internet of Things (IoT) technologies into their own products to facilitate direct-to-consumer replenishment. It's logical to assume therefore that most products in our lives will eventually be enabled with at least some degree of connectedness, intelligence and ability to self-replenish.

This new reality sets up an interesting conundrum for marketers. How do you sell laundry detergent to a piece of artificial intelligence that is programmed to default to a specific brand? If you're Budweiser, how do you appeal to the taste buds of a sensor that's buried in the guts of a refrigerator and programmed to reorder Corona? If you're New Balance, how do you reach the consumer whose Nike running shoes reorder their next-generation equivalent when they reach a certain level of wear? If you're Tesco, Walmart or Target, how do you get even a sliver of a market in which Amazon DRS lives inside most of the world's products? And how on earth do you reach the consumers of any of these products once those consumers no longer do the shopping themselves?

And as for Procter & Gamble's store-back approach? If consumers no longer need to pass through the detergent aisle of their grocery store, any marketing placed in those aisles is rendered as silent as the proverbial tree falling in the forest with no one there to hear it. In-store merchandising, coupon danglers, end caps, dump bins, point-of-purchase (POP) displays, shelf-edge videos and other conventional enticements will do little to appeal to the hundreds of connected and dispassionate devices tasked with managing our routine daily consumption.

Marketers across categories will soon have to reckon with a terribly unnerving question: How do they market to consumers along a path to purchase when that path no longer exists?

A Future
Artificially Sweetened

ASSUMING YOU LIVE in any developed consumer market, you've undoubtedly already encountered a chatbot, which is an interactive, artificially intelligent program that draws on cloud-based data to respond in real time to queries and conversation using natural-language processing. If you've ever called a company and connected to an automated call attendant that asks you a series of questions in order to guide your call, that's a low-grade chatbot.

While the term "chatbot" is relatively new, the idea of speaking to our computers isn't. It's captured our imaginations for decades. Movies and TV shows such as *Star Trek*, *2001: A Space Odyssey* and *Knight Rider* all played on our inherent human desire to anthropomorphize technology. Until recently, however, the ability to carry on fairly natural conversations with our technology has been limited. Anyone who has ever been reduced to yelling at an automated phone system that doesn't understand what they're saying will know what I mean. But recent breakthroughs in processing speed, cloud computing and natural-language processing have opened up tremendous opportunities for companies to begin employing chatbots for more complex functions and applications.

Chatbots may not eliminate 1-800 call centers altogether, at least not in the short term. In most cases, they will merely act as the front line of the customer service experience, reducing wait times for customer engagement and acting as triage for initial queries. Second, and as importantly, bots will also capture, index and eventually mine the data that comes from these interactions.

Over the course of time, as bots become increasingly sophisticated, the human versus bot distinction will likely fade. As Chris Messina, Uber's Developer Experience Lead, recently put it, "I'm less interested in whether a conversational service is provided by a human, bot, or some combination thereof. If I use these terms interchangeably, it's not unintentional. It's just that over an increasing period of time, computer-driven bots will become more human-feeling, to the point where the user can't detect the difference, and will interact with either human agent or computer bot in roughly the same interaction paradigm."[1]

Messina's notion that these strings of code might soon easily pass as human operators is commonly referred to as the Turing Test. Developed in the 1950s by Alan Turing, a computer programmer whose work was the subject of the 2014 film *The Imitation Game,* the test proposes that if after five minutes of interaction with an artificial intelligence the user cannot discern whether they are speaking with a computer or with a human being, the technology will have passed the test. In essence, the technology will have displayed intelligence equal to that of a human being.

SPEAK AND YE SHALL RECEIVE

ONE OF CHINA'S most beloved personalities is Xiaoice (pronounced Sh-ow-ice). Each day, millions of young Chinese people connect with her to share their photos, their stories and even the most intimate details of their lives, including career ups and downs and personal relationships. For some, Xiaoice is a shoulder to cry on; for others, she's a trusted confidante. Some have even confessed their love for her. Xiaoice returns their affections, remembering each and every one of her fans and their personal circumstances. She will often bring up life events from previous conversations and routinely asks how her friends are feeling or coping. She's even landed herself a job reporting the weather on one of China's largest daily news networks.

She's smart, empathetic, understanding and has a quirky sense of humor. In fact, Xiaoice really only has one discernable fault: she isn't real. That's right. She's a piece of interactive artificial intelligence (AI), commonly known as a chatbot, that was developed by Microsoft.

Xiaoice began as the result of a Microsoft hackathon and has become a central figure in Microsoft's exploration of how humans and AI interact. By mining scenarios from billions of online conversations, Xiaoice develops the capability to determine how best to respond to different user queries and situations. Users can engage her in playful banter, ask for news or information, have her set reminders and even translate conversations. According to Microsoft's managing director of Applications & Services, Yongdong Wang, "We can now claim that Xiaoice has entered a self-learning and self-growing loop. She is only going to get better."[2]

As bots march toward the Turing threshold, it seems inevitable that they will soon breach a line where, in our minds, they will cease to be mere pieces of software and become more like close personal confidants, standing at our beck and call.

The future of retail talks back

Facebook is one of the companies that have been expanding the role of chatbots beyond the call center. In April of 2016, at its F8 developer conference in San Francisco, Facebook CEO Mark Zuckerberg announced that the network would be assisting brands in creating chatbots on its fast-growing Messenger platform. The move will allow businesses to leverage Messenger to facilitate customer support, ecommerce sales and a host of other services.

Facebook's announcement signified its clear belief in two big ideas: first, that messaging would soon be the dominant online communication form, and second, that chatbots would eventually become the prevailing human-to-computer communication paradigm. Supporting Facebook's case was the fact that by as early as 2015 messaging apps had surpassed social networks in terms of monthly active users on phones[3] and was well on its way to overtaking email. WhatsApp, Facebook Messenger, WeChat and Viber are now attracting more users per month than Facebook, LinkedIn, Twitter and Instagram. Increasingly, social networks are morphing into chat networks.

Messaging also offers brands significant latitude with respect to the content they can build into the experience. Beyond text, it is now also possible for video, images and interactive content and payment platforms to be shared with shoppers. Messaging's instant nature along with its thread-based, archived format make it a very user-friendly and efficient means of communication.

Expanding the presence and role of chatbots also fed Facebook's broader commercial ambitions. The social network had been working feverishly to move the business-to-consumer relationship beyond benign "likes" and "shares" to more direct commerce in order to better allow brands to actually sell on Facebook. According to the network, Messenger gives brands the ability to connect to its 900 million–strong user base directly, instantly and, arguably, in their moments of greatest purchase intent—all, of course, without ever leaving Facebook's domain.

As for the bot universe, Facebook's announcement opened the floodgates, spawning an ever-growing landscape of bots capable of a myriad of services. Only two months after Facebook's announcement, more than eleven thousand bots were already up and running on Messenger.[4] And as a tech segment, more than $4 billion has already changed hands within the bot economy.

What this means for shoppers is that instead of having to download a particular brand's app or visit its website, they could simply open up Facebook Messenger, type the brand name into the search bar and almost instantly be connected to a chatbot. The bot would then guide the conversation, helping shoppers to narrow down the choices through a series of simple questions. Along the way, the bot could offer the alternatives that seem most appropriate for an individual consumer's needs.

As one might expect, brands have been quick to build bot-driven experiences on Facebook. A few of the many high-profile brands to jump in are American Express, Bank of America, Burger King, eBay and StubHub. Others are following fast. For example, Mondelez, the maker of Trident gum, Cadbury chocolates and other snacks, envisions a world where when you want one of its products, you simply type the product name into Facebook's Messenger search bar and you'll be instantly connected with an ordering bot. In other words, if you want more Oreos, simply say or type "Oreos" on Messenger, and Oreos cometh! An American Express demonstration showed that a customer who buys an airline ticket to New York online could later receive a notification from a bot via Messenger with a complimentary flight lounge pass, airport map and New York restaurant recommendations. In essence, the bot becomes an artificially intelligent concierge of sorts.

The personal digital assistant

In my 2013 book, *The Retail Revival,* I described a not-so-distant future in which each of us, as consumers, would operate with the ever-present help of virtual digital assistants. These assistants, I suggested, would not only anticipate our shopping needs, but would also make intelligent recommendations to fulfill them based on a knowledge of our preferences, personal relationships, physical location, budget and other considerations. They would eventually even execute transactions on our behalf and manage shipping and delivery without much intervention on our part, save perhaps for final go-ahead approval. I also believed that we would ultimately choose to subscribe to a particular trusted provider—be it Apple, Google, Amazon or another—and in doing so, literally open the floodgates of data, intelligence and personal information required to power these assistants to their full potential. These virtual assistants would, as I saw it, become the ever-present center of our consumer lives, our constant and trusted virtual companions. We might even feel a human level of emotional attachment to them.

At that time, many felt this dystopian vision of the future was ambitious to say the least and maybe even downright delusional. And I'll concede the reaction was understandable. Apple's Siri had only been introduced a few months earlier and was seen by most as being directionally exciting but still very functionally flawed, particularly when it came to natural speech recognition. Google's AI, called Now, had just been introduced in July of 2012 and was still quite narrow in its capabilities. It was easy in the early stages to dismiss much of this work as experimental at best.

For myself and others, however, the potential for AI to completely reshape our relationship with technology seemed abundantly clear. In fact, AI has progressed faster than most of us could have imagined. According to futurist Ray Kurzweil, by as early as 2029, computers will demonstrate a level of cognitive capability greater than *all human beings on Earth combined.* AI will make its way into almost every aspect of our daily lives. From the devices in our pockets to the cars we ride in and even the roads we drive on—almost everything you can imagine will be connected and imbued with some level of intelligence.

So, the notion that we will come to use and depend on our technology as trusted assistants is no longer speculation. Digital assistants are not only a reality, they're thought by many to be the next giant leap forward in how we interact online; they are potentially more significant than even the graphical user interface when it was originated in 1973. According to Microsoft CEO Satya Nadella, humanity stands at "the cusp of a new frontier that pairs the power of natural human language with advanced machine intelligence."[5]

While many chatbots today are built on a relatively narrow form of AI, structured to field specific queries or tasks, a host of companies and startups are racing to build what is known as artificial general intelligence, or AGI. It would allow for digital assistants that can handle an astonishing range of topics, functions and utilities. In fact, since 2011, Google, IBM, Yahoo, Intel, Apple and a few others have acquired more than thirty companies working in the field of advanced artificial intelligence. Google alone has acquired nine of them!

The advent of chatbots and digital assistants is leading us out of the ecommerce era and into the c-commerce era—*conversational commerce*, with Apple's Siri, Microsoft's Cortana, Google's Now and Amazon's Alexa all vying to become the pre-eminent brand of digital assistant. In a conversational reality, we will merely speak our needs and they will be fulfilled.

To date, one of the most compelling examples of this has been Amazon's Echo, a device introduced to the general market in 2015. At first glance, Echo looks like nothing more than a decent Bluetooth speaker. However, because the device runs on what Amazon calls Alexa Voice Service (AVS), it has many capabilities. Echo can be called upon for anything from providing news and information to controlling other connected devices in a home, like thermostats and lights.

Additionally, and this should come as little surprise, Echo can add items to a shopping list and even order products directly from—you guessed it—Amazon. In fact, the ease with which this is possible is scary. Simply ask Alexa to order you any given product—pens, for example. She will first look through your prior orders for matches. When she finds the closest match to your request, she'll offer it as a suggestion. She might say, "Bic, ultra Round Stic grip, ball pen." She'll then tell you what the price of the item is and ask if that's what you would like to order. By saying yes, your order is placed, paid for by the payment type on file and shipped to the address on account. Done!

By mid-2015, Amazon pushed Echo's potential to disrupt even further by releasing a "skills kit" that allows third-party developers to build new functions into Echo, enabling its own products to be operated by Echo's AVS. The company even created what it calls the Alexa Fund, a $100 million reserve "open to anyone with an innovative idea for how voice technology can improve customers' lives" and leverage the Alexa Voice

Service.[6] Once again, like almost everything else it does, Amazon will leverage the network effect to scale AVS in remarkably short order.

But assisting with our known, articulated consumer needs is only the first step for technologies such as Alexa, Siri and others. Soon, with enough user history and learning from masses of cloud-based, aggregated user data, digital assistants will become highly predictive about what we're likely to need or want. These recommendations will take many aspects of our lives into account: where we are, whom we're with, what we're doing as well as our known preferences and dislikes. They will suggest the best hotels to meet our needs, restaurants we'll enjoy and entertainment options that are likely to appeal. They'll search out deals we like, use our loyalty points wherever possible and even manage our household budgets. And we will trust them like we trust a family member. Perhaps even more.

> "Artificial intelligence will reach human levels by around 2029. Follow that out further to, say, 2045, we will have multiplied the intelligence, the human biological machine intelligence of our civilization a billion-fold." **RAY KURZWEIL**

But would consumers not find all this creepy? Not so much. In fact, "70% of US millennials, and 62% of millennials in the UK, say they would appreciate a brand or retailer using AI technology to show more interesting products; 72% and 64%, respectively, believe that as the technology develops, brands using AI will be able to accurately predict what they want."[7]

What is obvious is that AI is already developing into a primary battleground for companies such as Apple, Google, Amazon and Microsoft. Those who can create the deepest, most proficient and predictive AI coupled with the best user experience will, in essence, hold the keys to the store of the future.

This reality raises a couple of key questions. Between the devices in our lives that simply replenish our routine products as needed and the digital assistants that anticipate our contextual, moment-to-moment needs, will we ever need to go to a store again? And, even if we do, will that store need to be real?

10

Virtually There

AS A TEEN, Palmer Luckey developed an uncanny knack for hacking and upgrading the performance of gaming systems and hardware. A serial tinkerer, he made extra money buying broken smartphones on eBay, fixing and then reselling them. Along the way he also developed a keen fascination with virtual reality (VR) technology and its potential to make video games more immersive and experiential.

Frustrated with the limited capabilities of current VR hardware, he began buying and tweaking decommissioned military-style virtual reality gear to improve on its functionality. Between 2009 and 2011, while attending California State University, Luckey interned at the Institute for Creative Technologies at the University of Southern California. It was there that he iterated several versions of a device he called Oculus. And by 2012, using his parents' garage in Long Beach as a laboratory and combining inexpensive ocular lenses, mobile technology and a lighter headset form factor, Luckey developed a prototype of what many saw as a quantum improvement in the category.

The Oculus Rift virtual reality headset in use.
PHOTO COURTESY OF MARXENT

Oculus caught the attention of gaming entrepreneur Brendan Iribe, and in 2012, Luckey, Iribe and a small group of partners staged a Kickstarter campaign hoping to fund the technology to the next level of development. The initial goal was to raise $500,000, which got dialed back to $250,000 after Luckey became jittery about asking for too much. To fuel the campaign, they offered a developer version of the technology to anyone contributing three hundred dollars or more. To their collective amazement, the campaign raised an astonishing $2.4 million— almost ten times their goal. Oculus was not only funded, it was flush with development cash.

In the meantime, Luckey's invention had also captured the imagination of another young tech entrepreneur—one who only a decade earlier had launched his own rather successful startup and was looking for the next big platform on which to grow it.

Like Palmer Luckey, Mark Zuckerberg believed in the potential of virtual reality to reshape the future of online content. So much so, that on March 25, 2014, Facebook announced a definitive agreement to acquire Oculus VR Inc. for a total cash and stock sum of $2 billion. Luckey had gone from garage-tech geek to billionaire in a matter of six short years.

In announcing the deal, Zuckerberg affirmed his unyielding belief that virtual reality is the future for online experiences. While he acknowledged that gaming was the first obvious entry point for the technology, he went on to say:

> But this is just the start. After games, we're going to make Oculus a platform for many other experiences. Imagine enjoying a court side seat at a game, studying in a classroom of students and teachers all over the world or consulting with a doctor face-to-face—just by putting on goggles in your home.
>
> This is really a new communication platform. By feeling truly present, you can share unbounded spaces and experiences with the people in your life. Imagine sharing not just moments with your friends online, but entire experiences and adventures.[1]

Imagine a world where you could bring your friends along with you to shop in any store in the world. A world where the very concept of what a store is and how we shop could be completely reimagined. Where you could virtually visit the homes of celebrities and shop by checking out their wardrobes, wine cellars and refrigerators and instantly buy the things you find there. A world where you could see, smell and hear the people, places and things around you. An altered reality where you could converse naturally with manufacturers and brand representatives, even if they happened to speak a different language, via real-time translation! Envision being able to transport yourself to a point where the line between what is digital and what is real evaporates and no longer matters. This is the future of virtual reality shopping.

One of the pioneers creating this future is Amir Rubin, CEO and co-founder of Sixense, an early developer of virtual and augmented reality experiences. In fact, Palmer Luckey was barely onto solid foods when Rubin began working with the earliest virtual reality technologies. Despite his veteran status, Rubin remains evangelical in his excitement about VR's potential value.

His initial experience with VR dates back to 1994 when he became involved in the creation of VR simulations for the U.S. and Israeli militaries, which companies such as Lockheed Martin continue to use today. By developing tremendously lifelike, immersive situations across a variety of combat scenarios, Rubin gave soldiers the ability to safely rehearse their skills for the deadliest of situations. These immersive moments, he believed, could completely transform how we learn, interact and ultimately benefit from technology.

But timing is everything, and he failed to find mainstream commercial interest until more than a decade later. In 2007, Rubin and a partner, Avi Arad, former CEO of Marvel Studios, saw the first Nintendo Wii being used, and in that moment it became clear to both of them that the world was ready for the immersive experiences that virtual reality could deliver. It was then that they co-founded Sixense with the goal of creating completely lifelike experiences that were almost indistinguishable from reality. This intense level of immersion is what Rubin and other VR technologists refer to as *presence*—the absolute and visceral sense that the situation you're in is real in every respect.

Reinventing the ecommerce experience

Beyond the novelty of the VR experience, is there a business case for VR shopping? In fact, there is. Consider that online shopping today comes with absolutely unsustainable levels of product returns. In the U.K. alone, online returns are estimated to cost retailers approximately £20 billion annually.[2] And in 2014, total returns in the U.S. were 8.89 percent of all retail sales, totaling more than $280 billion in lost sales[3]—a number that continues to grow along with ecommerce. It's these returns, more than anything else, that bombard the bottom lines of pure-play online retailers and call into question their long-term viability.

Much of the problem stems from shoppers' inherent inability to fully understand what they're buying online until they receive it. Virtual reality has the potential to bridge this experiential gap by allowing shoppers to literally interact with products before buying them, instead of relying solely on text descriptions, images or even video. Rubin notes, "We believe people deserve to go back to the good old days." He continues, "The days when you could try a product before buying it." In Rubin's view, "VR can give consumers a new level of confidence in their purchase—something they can't get today when shopping online."[4]

For example, Rubin describes a virtual experience his company recently designed for a drone manufacturer. It allows shoppers to test-fly various models of drone in different simulated conditions, such as indoors and outdoors or calm and windy conditions. The immersive, hands-on experience, coupled with the ability to replicate different user environments, enabled shoppers to truly understand what they were getting before they bought it. Consequently, as you'd expect, the drone manufacturer's sales and customer satisfaction both rose.[5]

This potential for businesses to transport shoppers to a new and more immersive level of engagement with their products and services has prompted significant levels of experimentation in the VR space. Marriott Hotels, for example, recently launched what it calls VRoom Service, a new initiative in partnership with Samsung. Using the Marriott mobile app, guests of the chain's hotels can request delivery of a virtual reality headset to their room. Headsets come preloaded with three VR Postcards, specially filmed travel logs that provide an immersive glimpse into such unique and exotic places as Rwanda, Beijing or the peaks of the Andes Mountains. Guests can be virtually transported to unique destinations from the comfort of their Marriott room. In each postcard, users accompany a real traveler who shares personal stories about the place they're trekking in. Compare this experience to clicking through a series of static pictures on a travel website and you can begin to appreciate why the travel industry has been one of the first-movers in adopting VR.

In the automobile market, luxury brand Audi, in conjunction with Samsung, recently launched its virtual test drive at the flagship Audi City showroom in London. The experience allows customers interested in the new Audi TT the opportunity to take a virtual drive, seeing, hearing and experiencing the vehicle while being whipped around a racetrack by Audi TT designer Jürgen Löffler. Stand this experience up against the last ho-hum test drive you took and it becomes obvious why other automakers, such as Volvo, have followed suit with their own virtual test drives.

In 2016, GM's luxury brand, Cadillac, went a bold step further, announcing that it would convert some of its physical dealerships into entirely virtual ones. Dubbed Project Pinnacle, the initiative allows dealers to showcase a wide variety of vehicles without maintaining an extensive physical inventory—a cost that has always weighed heavily on auto dealers. Shoppers can learn about and even test-drive vehicles virtually and then, once

The Lowe's HoloRoom Virtual Reality Design Space.
PHOTO COURTESY OF MARXENT

they've narrowed their choice, they can drive an actual test vehicle of the same make and model.

Meanwhile, in Australia, eBay partnered with department store brand Myer to create a virtual shopping experience using a functionality eBay calls Sight Search. Simply by training their gaze on certain products within the virtual environment, users can navigate the store's selection and receive layers of product information and visual media about them.

Increasingly, brands and retailers are awakening to the potential for virtual reality not only to enhance physical experiences but, perhaps more critically, to replace them entirely. Beck Besecker, CEO of Marxent, a leader in developing consumer-facing VR experiences, suggests that the technology is moving at a blinding speed. Besecker, whose company has staged VR experiences for key retail projects such as Lowe's Home Improvement's virtual reality kitchen and bath renovation system called

HoloRoom, believes that soon just about any company could possess the tools to produce its own VR content. "Just like Apple enabled people to create apps, we see that people will be able to create VR experiences,"[6] he says.

The user experience associated with VR is also going to become increasingly lifelike as the devices we use to experience it become more powerful and optimized. By 2020, Rubin estimates there will be at least 1 billion VR devices in the market. These devices, he believes, will have the capacity to work with a dramatically higher level of content resolution, thereby delivering even more lifelike images and realistic experiences—experiences that border on being indistinguishable from reality.

Good vibrations

Far from the solitary point-and-click ecommerce experience of today, we will soon be able to transport ourselves and our friends anywhere we wish to shop. We will take virtual vacations and bring home real-world products. We will interact with virtual salespeople, who will bring an endless assortment of products that we can try before we buy. And if Katherine Kuchenbecker has anything to do with it, we will also be able to touch and feel every product in the virtual world.

Kuchenbecker is an associate professor of mechanical engineering at Penn State University. She and her research team have been working for the better part of a decade developing a technology she calls haptography, or haptic photography. She explains, "We record what a person feels as they touch the real object, either clicking a real button or dragging a tool across a real texture, and use a computer program we've designed to analyze it and distill it out into the essence of that touch experience."[7] So, by creating a haptic profile of different materials, objects and surfaces, their unique properties can then be

This haptographic device allows users
to replicate the feeling of virtual 3D objects.

HEATHER CULBERTSON/KATHERINE J. KUCHENBECKER

converted into vibrations that can be felt through a specially designed stylus.

In one example, a device is used to capture the specific haptic properties of a piece of canvas, which are later translated into a mathematical model that's programmed into a computer. When you move a specially developed stylus across a glide pad on the computer, the vibrations that are transmitted reproduce the exact feeling of the canvas. In another example, Kuchenbecker and her team use a similar process to give dental students the ability to practice detecting cavities by simulating, exactly, the feeling of probing the different hardnesses on the surface of a tooth with a dental instrument. Other examples include putting on specially designed gloves and other wearables that register haptic feedback.

In a 2013 TED Talk, Kuchenbecker details a number of potential uses for haptography, and chief among them is online shopping. As she points out, the inability to touch and feel the products we shop for online has, from the beginning, been one of the most significant drawbacks for ecommerce, especially in the apparel and furniture categories. We know that how textiles and other materials feel is critical to our decision-making process and our ultimate satisfaction with the product, and this inability to touch these products—particularly clothing—has resulted in extraordinary rates of product returns. But imagine sitting in the comfort of your own home while shopping virtually for fine furniture in a store in Milan, where you can not only see the products and speak to the salespeople but you can also reach out and feel the products you're considering. Imagine how much more confident you'd be in your purchase decision.

When I asked Kuchenbecker what her ideal future for this technology looks like, she quite plainly said, "The next step is to get rid of the stylus." She envisions a world where our natural instinct to touch and feel is baked directly into the devices and platforms we use to access the web—a world where we can touch and feel the virtual. So, if you think Amazon is deadly today, imagine a future where Amazon ceases to be a digital catalog and instead becomes an expansive virtual world that you can step into. A place where you can see, feel and interact with any product on the face of the Earth. A reality in which you can actually try products before you buy them.

David Edwards smells

It's not a long way from Penn State to Harvard. Similarly, it's not a huge intellectual leap to imagine that if we may soon be able to touch and feel the things we see online, we may also be able to perceive their other sensual attributes. Professor David Edwards, a biomedical engineer by trade, shares this vision of the future. In fact, it's a pursuit that led him in 2014 to launch a technology called the oPhone. A small, connected device powered by a mobile app called oSnap, the oPhone allows users to send and receive a range of individual or combined scent messages (oNotes). The endgame for Edwards is to create what he terms the iTunes of scent, a place where books, music, media and other content can be augmented by olfactory information.

While it's easy to imagine all the sinister and smelly practical jokes this device would allow for, one can't help pondering the more serious commercial applications. But to do so we need to first appreciate the role that smell plays in our consumer lives.

While our noses contain only about half as many scent receptors as those of our canine friends, a remarkable proportion of our thoughts, feelings and perceptions about the world around us are centered in our olfactory capability. In fact, our deepest memories of people, places and things are most often primarily tied to scent above all other senses. In other words, long after the sight or sound of something fades, its scent may linger on in our deepest memory.

One only has to imagine the aroma of coffee brewing in the morning, the smell of leaves burning in the fall or the scent of a brand-new car to recognize just how much our nose knows. This isn't accidental. In fact, it's a miracle of physiological design and it has been instrumental in our success as a species. Science explains it as follows: "The limbic system comprises a set of structures within the brain that are regarded by scientists as playing a major role in controlling mood, memory, behavior and emotion. It is often regarded as being the old, or primitive, part of the brain, because these same structures were present within the brains of the very first mammals. Knowing this helps us to understand why smell plays such an important role in memory, mood and emotion."[8]

Given the role that our sense of smell plays in perception, it follows that it also powerfully influences the choices we make, from the restaurants we eat in, to the car we buy, to the person we choose as a mate.

While Edwards admits that the technology is still very much in the nascent stages, he remains confident that scent will indeed become information that gets transmitted, just like any other data. In an interview with *The New Yorker,* Edwards said, "Right now, nobody's waking up at 3 A.M. saying, 'I really want to send a scent message.' But one day they will."[9]

One can't help but wonder how much more powerful our online shopping experiences might be if we could not only see and feel products but also smell them. Imagine perceiving the scent of the leather sofa you're considering, or being able to sample various bouquets of wine online before making a selection. Scent could very well be the ultimate digital content that tips the scales in favor of one product or business over another.

A Whole
New Reality

THE COMMUNITY OF Rhodes, Australia, was on edge. The quiet suburb of Sydney was being overrun with outsiders. According to one resident, "The place is in complete chaos with crowds of well over 1,000 per night. There is a massive level of noise after midnight, uncontrollable traffic, excessive rubbish, smokers, drunk people, people who are 'camping' in the site, and even people peddling mobile phone chargers."[1] The problem became so significant in fact that Helen McCaffrey, mayor of Canada Bay, the local government area in which Rhodes is located, had to call in extra rangers and order extra waste collection. According to the report, police were forced to disperse the crowd with threats of two-hundred-dollar loitering fines.

Rhodes, it seemed, was in crisis. But contrary to what you might think, the problems in Rhodes were not the result of economic strife or social unrest, nor of urban decay or illicit drug trade. The cause of Rhodes' nightly calamity was Pokémon Go, a tech-heavy take on the epic Pokémon franchise, which dates back to 1996 and includes toys, video games, TV shows and trading cards, among other things. The location-based game leads players, or "trainers" as they are called, on a journey to find, capture, collect and even trade virtual creatures called Pokémon.

To call Pokémon Go a craze doesn't really characterize it properly. It was nothing short of a global mania. By July of 2016, research firm SimilarWeb reported that Go had more daily Android app users than Twitter and was quickly closing in on Snapchat. Players were spending an average of forty-three minutes per day on Go—more than WhatsApp, Instagram or Snapchat. Social media firm Spredfast reported that in the week following its release, Pokémon Go generated more tweets than Brexit did during the week of the U.K. referendum. By late July, Apple confirmed that Pokémon Go had more first-week downloads than any other app in history.

As it turned out, the tiny area of Rhodes was located at the intersection of three prolific PokéStops containing hundreds of virtual characters, many of them very rare. Thus, hordes of players were descending on the community each day in an effort to capture their elusive quarry and at the same time bringing much grief to the residents of Rhodes.

You may be wondering what any of this has to do with the future of retail. As it turns out, a lot. Because beyond simply being a tremendously successful game, Pokémon Go managed to do what no other app had managed to. It brought augmented reality (AR) technology to a mass consumer audience on a global scale.

In the simplest of terms, AR allows us to superimpose digital content onto the physical world around us. And while virtual reality has been stealing headlines of late, many believe that its close cousin, augmented reality, will have a more profound impact on consumers. It's estimated that AR will become a $90 billion market by as early as 2020.

Magic Leap's mixed reality demonstration
of a leaping whale in a gymnasium.

IMAGE COURTESY OF MAGIC LEAP

As far back as 2009, I was following such companies as Layar and Blippar and their work to leverage AR with brands and retailers. IKEA has employed this technology to allow users to visualize items from its catalogs in their own homes. Lego has used AR to show the contents of its boxed Lego sets to children in its stores. And building materials manufacturers have adopted AR to let shoppers visualize new products overlaid onto their existing spaces and surfaces. AR has proven that it can add enormous value in a wide variety of situations. So, while brands and technologists have been experimenting with AR for the better part of a decade, it took Pokémon Go to catapult augmented reality to the forefront of consumer awareness.

A leap of faith

No other company in the field has managed to generate more mystery, media or venture money than Magic Leap. Founded in 2010, it describes itself as a "computing platform that will enable you to seamlessly combine and experience your digital and physical lives."[2]

Unlike augmented reality, which are technologies that simply produce digital content on a device and then appear to overlay it onto the physical world via the device's camera, Magic Leap employs what founder Rony Abovitz calls mixed reality (MR). Using light field technology—the same technology used to create holograms—MR feeds digital inputs through the eyes to the brain and literally tricks it into believing that what it's seeing is real. Essentially, by making your brain the computer processor, MR can deliver cinematic-quality experiences that exceed anything that we've ever known before. In essence, Magic Leap has developed a means of delivering holographic images directly to users via their brains!

The company made waves in 2015 when it published a mocked-up demonstration video showing a school gymnasium filled with kids. Suddenly a life-sized whale breached through the gym floor, rose twenty feet in the air and crashed back down with a massive splash! Needless to say, the students and anyone who saw the video were amazed.

Magic Leap's investor list includes a number of A-list companies, such as Alibaba, Google, Qualcomm, Andreessen Horowitz and Warner Bros., among others. And if capital investment is any sort of proxy for the perceived potential for a technology or market, it's worth noting that Magic Leap has raised almost $4 billion and, as of late 2016, had yet to release a single product. That said, many believe that its technology has the potential to deliver a technological breakthrough as significant as the Internet itself.

Although the company has been notoriously secretive about what its final product will look like, tech columnists around the world have been attempting to follow the breadcrumbs of their announcements, patent filings and executive hires to piece together a sense of what might be going on inside the tent. One tech media writer suggested it's likely to be a "Google Glass on steroids that can seamlessly blend computer-generated graphics with the real world. A headset packed with fiber optic projectors, crazy lenses, and loads of cameras. An augmented reality that you'll actually believe in."[3]

To get a sense of the degree to which Magic Leap might change our online experiences, one only has to take a look at the key points from its recent patent filing:

→ No physical computer or device of any kind would be required except for the glasses and a small pocket pack.
→ Virtual controllers would alleviate the need for physical controllers. Keyboards and other interfaces can appear anywhere the user wishes.
→ Mapping technology would allow virtual objects to be placed in real-world spaces.
→ Friends, family and others may appear in the room with you, making it possible to have interactive classes, workshops or any other social experience. You will see them and they will see you.
→ Reviews, ratings, comments can appear over products.
→ Shopping cart handles become their own computer interface.
→ Products in-store or at home may become their own interactive advertisements.
→ Companies could stage virtual demonstrations of their products.

Magic Leap has also incorporated into its patent filing what it calls "haptic gloves," connected gloves that deliver vibrational feedback to create the sensation of touching and feeling virtual objects. It's a feature that will no doubt delight haptography pioneer Katherine Kuchenbecker!

Even if we apply a 50 percent B.S. factor to this list, Magic Leap is still likely to be mind-bending. And to illustrate just how differently Magic Leap may be approaching the idea of shopping, its chief marketing officer, Brian Wallace, describes an application the company is working on called Look-Buy. According to

Wallace, it's a system of commerce in which you could buy the things around you simply by looking at them. "So, I'm looking at your sweater," Wallace says, "and I'm like, 'Wow, it's really nice.' My system recognizes that I'm looking at your sweater; Alibaba pops up, recognizes that, makes me an offer and says if you buy it now you get 10 percent off. I also look down and I can see myself in it."[4] Then, Wallace says, with a simple acknowledgment, it can be purchased and paid for.

So, as difficult as it might be to imagine, you will someday very soon be able to shop for anything, wherever you are. If you want to view a full-sized Porsche 911 in the comfort of your living room, you will do so. If you want to visit the Champs-Élysées on your lunch break and pick up a dress to wear to next weekend's wedding, you will go, shop and return without ever leaving your desk. If you and your family want to visit the Grand Canyon together, you will do so, without ever setting foot in a plane. In the future, wherever you are, whatever you want, it will be virtually yours.

If the shoe fits, buy it

So, it's very clear that we're rapidly advancing into a world where every aspect of a shopping journey can and will be instant, immersive, customized, sensory and informed with artificial intelligence.

Regrettably, what we cannot do (not yet anyway) is physically try items on before we buy them. This inability to properly fit items pre-purchase is one of the online apparel industry's most significant problems and leads to a phenomenon known as "size sampling"—ordering several different sizes of the same item but keeping only what fits and sending the rest back. In fact, of the total volume of apparel sold online, an estimated 25 to 40 percent is returned to retailers, which represents a staggering cost to those businesses. Moreover, the hassle for online shoppers creates a significant sticking point for online apparel sales growth.

Soon, however, this issue of fit will not even register as a concern for either the retailer or the shopper. Everything you are shown and everything you buy, whether on Facebook or in a virtual world, will fit you well. In fact, it's entirely likely that the items offered to you will be precurated, not only to fit you but also to best reflect your personal style and fashion sense.

This is the vision that Romney Evans and his team at True Fit are turning into a reality. It began when Evans was working at the Boston-based consulting firm Innosight, a firm founded by Clayton Christensen, author of *The Innovator's Dilemma*, a book also known as The New Testament in Silicon Valley. The book and Christensen's consultancy focus on the concept of disruptive technologies and how companies and inventors can make dramatic improvements to markets with game-changing innovation. "While I was working there," Evans says, "I was thinking about all those frameworks and one day was out shopping with my wife and she was trying on clothes and she tried on probably a dozen pairs of jeans; she bought nothing, she left disappointed and felt bad about herself, and for me I just thought, 'Man, this is really painful.' Is it really this difficult for everybody?" he wondered. "And that's when I first started thinking, wouldn't it be cool if you could go online and enter some information about yourself and have it tell you which items were going to fit you well, which items wouldn't and what size to buy."[5]

The experience prompted him to co-found True Fit, a Massachusetts-based startup company that has developed what it calls "the first-ever Genome™ for apparel and footwear," a colossal pool of technical product data from approximately ten thousand footwear and apparel brands matched against the style and fit preferences of a community of more than 30 million registered users worldwide. The result is an elegant and easy-to-use recommendation engine for style and fit that resides within the retailer's own website. Customers wondering if a product will fit them simply enter a few pieces of information about other styles and sizes they wear, and True Fit then makes a recommendation based on other customer and technical data. The more users that interact with the engine, the smarter it becomes and the better it ultimately works.

"We can give you the experience as though you're walking into a department store and everything that doesn't fit you just disappears," says Evans. "And what floats to the top are all the items you are likely to love and keep. Now the consumer can focus on the fun part of shopping which they love, which is the exploration of those items."

Shopping online, he says, "becomes a much more dramatic problem if you are limited by the form factor of mobile, where you can't fit all twenty selections on one screen as easily and you've got to keep paging through all these results."[6] It becomes even more important, Evans says, to display the items that are most likely to fit the shopper's body well.

While True Fit isn't the only company working toward a solution to the fit problem, I have to say it's among the first I've encountered that is able to point to legitimate commercial results. Its most recent trials, Evans points out, have yielded retailers an average 5 percent increase in net incremental revenue over a pre–True Fit baseline and also recorded dramatic reductions in the percentage of returns. As True Fit becomes increasingly robust with data, Evans sees its utility evolving to the point where it will begin actively curating fashion choices for its users based on fit and style, as well as purchase data. Your own personal algorithm will follow you wherever you go online and present you with only the things that are most ideal for you.

The future of shopping will fit perfectly.

12

Baby, You Can
Print My Car

A FASTER HORSE, the 2015 documentary directed by David Gelb, chronicles the painstaking journeys of Ford's design and production teams as they brought the fiftieth anniversary version of the company's iconic Mustang to market. The film details the astounding amount of time, money and energy that goes into the production of an automobile. It also captures the extraordinary pressure involved in such a high-stakes venture. Fortunately for Mustang lovers, *A Faster Horse* ends happily. The anniversary-edition car was not only released to the market on time, but even its most discerning fans giddily received it. Success.

And so it is in most manufacturing scenarios: tremendously long design processes followed by extraordinary and costly engineering work, coupled with lengthy production ramp up and laden with massive upfront capital investment and risk. And if it all goes well (and that's a big IF), the manufacturer produces thousands or millions of units of its product, which it ships at a modest profit to a network of dealers. And for all that combined effort, car buyers receive a product that is, by definition, a compromise, a product built to adequately satisfy the widest possible range of tastes and preferences without being perfectly designed for anyone.

This is not how things work at Local Motors. Unlike Ford, Local Motors has no storied history, no iconic founder, no emblematic brand beloved by car enthusiasts and no racing pedigree. What Local Motors does have, however, is the ability to three-dimensionally (3D) print an automobile in a matter of hours! That's right, I said hours.

Founded in 2007, Local Motors is an American manufacturing company focused on the low-volume production of automobiles and a variety of other products. Headquartered in Phoenix, the company was the brainchild of John (Jay) Rogers Jr., who started to make a name for himself in 2011 when Local Motors began producing completely crowd-source-designed, road-legal rally fighter automobiles, one of which was featured on the TV show *Jay Leno's Garage*.

In 2014, over forty-four hours, Local Motors produced the world's first crowd-sourced, 3D printed automobile. Using a printing method called big area additive manufacturing, or BAAM, Local Motors managed to print an entire vehicle's chassis and body as one, eliminating more than twenty thousand typical auto parts in the process. Mitchell Menaker, the company's chief sales officer, says, "We've done a rally fighter that is still produced which was the world's first co-created vehicle done about 5 years ago. We brought that car from challenge to market in under 12 months." By contrast he points out, "It takes the typical OEM [original equipment manufacturer] 6 to 8 years to do the comparable thing and usually about a billion dollars to bring the car to market."[1]

Contrary to what its name might suggest, Local Motors is neither local in scale nor a car company in scope. In fact, the company has undertaken manufacturing challenges for a variety

Designer Edgar Sarmiento in the 3D printed Olli bus.
IMAGE COURTESY OF LOCAL MOTORS

of companies and products, including appliances for GE and a quadcopter drone for Airbus. Rogers and his team have plans to establish dozens of mini-manufacturing sites around the world.

Local's uniqueness isn't limited to its 3D printing manufacturing approach. It also takes a very different approach to design. "We actually have a community that is 60 thousand people strong in 123 countries," Menaker says. "Whether you are an amateur designer, an enthusiast, a hobbyist, an engineer, a rocket scientist, whatever you happen to be, you get to go ahead and be creative on our site by everything from posting products, posting blogs or participating in one of our challenges."[2]

It was within Local's creative community that Edgar Sarmiento, a twenty-four-year-old industrial designer from Bogotá, Colombia, saw an opportunity to satisfy his love for product development. Sarmiento submitted his design for a self-driving electric minibus for mass transit usage, and it was chosen by Local to go to prototype. In return, he received a check for twenty thousand dollars and will also collect an undisclosed royalty from sales of the Olli, as it has been named. Menaker shares only that based on sales inquiries about the Olli, it's conceivable that Sarmiento may be able to retire young. "Ford or GM," he says, "wouldn't have taken this young man's phone call."

In Menaker's vision of the future, the customer will come in to the showroom in the morning, help design their vehicle over coffee, have it printed that day and drive it home that evening. Beyond the unique approach to making cars, Local Motors also intends to recycle entire vehicles. "You'll be able to drive your vehicle, come back two years from now, trade your vehicle in and we'll be able to melt your car down and make a whole new vehicle out of it," Menaker says.

This incredible potential for technology to change the way we manufacture things prompts one to wonder when we are likely to see 3D printing become a standard mode of production for the kinds of products we buy each day. When our clothing, accessories and footwear, for example, might be completely bespoke and printed just for us. One hint at such a future came from Nike Chief Operating Officer Eric Sprunk in October 2015. Sprunk was participating in a panel discussion at the GeekWire Summit when he was asked whether he foresaw a future in which Nike customers would be able to print their products at home. To the surprise of many, Sprunk not only affirmed this potential future but went on to say, "Do I envision a future where [Nike] might still own the file, from an IP perspective... and you can manufacture that either in your home or we will do it for you at our store? Oh yeah, that's not that far away."[3]

Let's be clear. This wasn't some fanatical 3D printing evangelist or exuberant startup retailer talking. This was the chief operating officer of a Fortune 500 brand hinting at an on-demand, fully individualized supply chain almost wholly controlled by consumers—and not as though it was science fiction but like it was just around the corner.

Impossible, right?

Not at all, according to Joe DeSimone. And he ought to know. He's a decorated American chemist, one of fewer than twenty people to be elected to all three branches of the National Academies (medicine, sciences and engineering) and a long-standing professor of chemistry at the University of North Carolina–Chapel Hill. DeSimone, as it turns out, is also a pioneer who is completely revolutionizing manufacturing.

DeSimone's company, Carbon, has developed a printing technology called continuous liquid interface production, or CLIP for short. Unlike conventional 3D printing technologies that create objects by creating layers of material, usually hard plastics, Carbon's process produces incredibly complex objects using ultraviolet light to catalyze resins continuously and at an exponentially faster pace. The best way to describe it, for anyone who saw the *Terminator* films, is that just like the scene in which the evil T-1000 robot rises out of a puddle of future-goo and rapidly reforms itself, Carbon's process makes fully finished objects very similarly rise rapidly out of a container of resin in their finished form.

> "Make no mistake, 3D printing is nothing short of a new industrial revolution that also holds potential for major innovation in terms of economic models, not least via on-demand production." **PASCAL MORAND**

"It's a breakthrough that's going to enable 3D manufacturing," DeSimone says. He continues: "3D manufacturing is something that people have been talking about for a while. You know,

I think there was a lot of excitement, and almost every Fortune 500 company that makes a physical object started thinking about the impact of a digital device for fabricating objects, but I think everyone basically shelved their plans because the products that come out of the printer, really are pretty crappy and it's not being done at a speed or an economics that matter either."[4]

Carbon's process is, however, designed to enable enterprise-level businesses to rapidly fabricate completely functional, dynamic and high-quality products for consumers on a bespoke basis. "It allows complex things and allows us to make things very quickly, and so having final parts, parts that have properties to be used as functional parts and doing it at game-changing speeds, is the technological breakthrough that I think is going to trigger the full-blown 3D manufacturing sector to emerge."[5]

As for Nike's vision of bespoke shoemaking using 3D printing, DeSimone offered that, "Every athletic footwear company has been trying to enable their designs and their aspirations for bespoke footwear to go forward, and they've been saddled with the legacy technology. On that backdrop, we've been in the midst of a broad discussion about market entry and we're going to be locking up with a specific shoe company in a really exciting way that's very consumer facing."[6] I sensed that this was DeSimone's cautious way of saying, *yes, your customized running shoes will soon be printed and waiting for you to pick them up.*

As he contemplates the magnitude of this technology, DeSimone says, "The way I look at it is, the ability to fabricate stuff has been the prowess and ownership of the rich and powerful. And to put really powerful fabrication tools that are cost effective into the hands of smaller companies and entrepreneurs, I think that's going to be empowering, in a really significant way, to have people's own ideas get translated into a physical object."[7]

What all this adds up to is a new industrial revolution unlike anything we've seen before. Technology is not only changing the way we shop, but also the way products are created. In the not-too-distant future, companies will be able to create fully bespoke, high-quality products at a scale and cost that was previously impossible. Small manufacturers will also be able to use these advanced technologies to effectively compete with their larger rivals. And consumers will have the potential to become co-designers and even small-scale manufacturers in their own right. It will be a complete rethinking of the entire supply chain—and it will change the face of both retail and manufacturing forever.

Is Retail Dead?

SO, WHEN I step back and look at this bigger picture, what is clear to me is that Andreessen's comments were not just the bluster of a tech luminary making off-the-cuff predictions. He has a remarkably well-supported point and it appears to be playing out around us more and more each day. Software, if not completely devouring retail, is clearly kicking the living crap out of it. Ecommerce as we know it today is only the beginning of a future retail state that will be simply astounding. And in a post-digital world, consumers will no longer marvel at technology but simply come to expect it and the benefits that come with it. Any business stuck in the mid-digital era will look Dickensian.

In the face of this reality, and everything that has changed over the past quarter century, how on earth can retail—a business model thousands of years old—presume to carry on as though it's business as usual?

In the cold light of the twenty-first century, one has to honestly ask, is Marc Andreessen right? Are we indeed seeing the complete disintegration of retail as a concept and the store as its central operating model? Is it conceivable that stores as we know them will become virtual places that I can visit without ever leaving home? Will we soon live in a world where everything we own comes to our door via drone copter? Will the devices in our lives or even products themselves determine what we get, when we get it and from whom? Indeed, will we the consumers become the designers and co-producers of much of what we buy and simply print it on demand? And moreover, as a result of all these changes, will brick-and-mortar stores and malls and main streets become abandoned monoliths of a different age? Will tumbleweeds blow down the high streets of major cities?

In other words, is retail dead?

The answer is unequivocally no. Retail is not dead. While everything I've described will almost certainly come to pass in some manner, its net effect will not be the death of retail. Not even close. In fact, what's about to happen is infinitely more complex, momentous, inspired and amazing.

PART

3

THE STORE IS MEDIA

14

The Human Elements of Retail

CONNECTED DEVICES WILL begin to monitor, manage and even control more and more of our purchase activity. Technology will allow us to shop virtually and in a wholly immersive way. Virtual reality will take us wherever we want, whenever we want. Augmented reality will turn the world around us into a lifelike store, wherever we happen to be at that moment. If you want to buy Kanye West's new album, you may very well be able to do so while hanging out and listening to it with a virtual representation of Kanye himself. I'll leave it to the reader to decide if that's a selling point.

There is also little question that we will very naturally speak to our AI-powered assistants and they will look after getting us whatever we desire. All these things are quite certain. But does the inevitability of this future negate the need for physical shopping spaces? Will technology usurp the live shopping experience?

I believe that the answer is no. As long as humans shop for reasons beyond the mere acquisition of things, physical retail spaces will remain relevant. In fact, as we become increasingly tethered to technology they will become even more valuable, more cherished, as our hunger for visceral and emotionally connected experiences will intensify. The simple fact is that, at its core, shopping is a human activity. It's a need that's been baked into humanity, stretching back to our most distant history as hunters and gatherers.

From the Roman marketplace of 400 BC to the grand department stores of Paris and London to New York's Fifth Avenue, we have shopped through the ages for a multitude of reasons beyond the mere acquisition of goods. Shopping appeals to our deepest subconscious needs and goes deep within our psyche.

We saw this profoundly after the 9/11 terrorist attacks in the United States. While many economists anticipated a significant drop in consumer activity, which would have been understandable given the scale and nature of the tragedy, the exact opposite happened. Consumers bought more, much more. It's a phenomenon psychologists call *mortality salience*—the realization of one's own impermanence—and it drives an increased desire for goods and services that "provide people with a sense of comfort and stability."[1]

We shop to discover

Shopping, at its best, always holds the hope of profound moments of discovery. The thrill of the hunt and the uncovering of treasure affect us, as humans, on multiple levels.

Ironically, as our lives become more hyperconnected by technology and driven by data, the world around us becomes less discoverable and the odds of encountering things in an unanticipated way become much slimmer. That may sound counterintuitive but it's a fact.

Increasingly, the people, places and things that make it into our field of awareness are being driven by data and predetermined algorithmically. Social networks such as Facebook don't expand our circle of friends; they actually contract it by winding us more tightly in relation to information, products, events and people that we "like" and shutting the door on those people, places and things that we're less inclined toward. Before too long, Facebook begins to act like an echo chamber of our own thoughts, beliefs, likes and dislikes, all bouncing back at us from people just like us.

Similarly, Netflix doesn't expand our viewing universe; it contracts it by recommending shows and movies similar to the ones we just enjoyed. Spotify doesn't broaden our musical tastes; it narrows them by serving us more songs like the one we just added to a playlist. And dating sites don't attempt to bring uniquely different people together to create magic. They match people, like pairs of socks, in the interest of compatibility.

Retail is no different.

My wife and I once bought outdoor furniture at Costco. Twice a week for a full year following the purchase, we received outdoor furniture offers from Costco. In another case, I bought a part for my car from eBay. Years later, I'm still receiving notifications about identical items. It's illogical, of course, for these companies to simply deluge their customers with more offers for products they've just purchased, but it stands as a clear example of how data on its own can be a very blunt and ineffective instrument. It's as though serendipity is dead and our own data is the smoking gun!

Some would argue that, despite their imperfections, these sorts of algorithmic recommendations are a welcome alternative to the nauseating levels of mass advertising that have plagued us for the better part of a century. While I agree that no one needs more mass marketing, it's also true that an overly data-centric approach to retail has an almost anesthetizing effect on our shopping experiences, increasingly sapping them of the exhilaration that accidental discovery can provide.

The true joy of shopping lies in the delicate balance of relevance and randomness. While it's true that as shoppers we appreciate being exposed to things that appeal to our conscious needs and preferences, we also crave the surprise and delight of encountering shops we had no idea we'd love, products we didn't know existed and experiences that come out of nowhere to surprise and enchant us. Physical stores can and should be these enchanted places. And data, no matter how good it is, can never replicate the experience of genuine discovery.

We shop because it's social

We may complain about the crowds of people we encounter when we go shopping, but our innate human response to crowds is quite the opposite. We subconsciously seek them out.

Have you ever noticed that a store can sit empty for several minutes but as soon as a few shoppers enter, more people seem immediately drawn to the space? In fact, given an equal choice between two shops—one empty and one with people in it—we will almost always go where others are gathered. This is the social essence of shopping in a nutshell. Crowds are the clearest and most immediate form of *social proof*, a reality that hasn't changed since we climbed down from the trees tens of thousands of years ago. The presence of others in a space remains our best primal indicator that something of value is going on there.

Most of us can relate to the adrenaline rush of being in a mall or a store and happening upon a feeding frenzy of shopper activity; it's that feeling of excitement you experience when you sense that something big is going down. How else could you possibly explain the mayhem that Black Friday sales have become? Crowds, excitement and buzz are all intoxicating.

Apple has, almost from the beginning, been the master of creating this sort of human electricity in its physical locations. Most of us can recall the images of lineups stretching around

Thousands of shoppers line up for blocks to attend
the Apple store's launch of the iPhone 6 in New York City.
ROBERT CICCHETTI

city blocks as people waited for new iPhones. Yet, even Apple recognized that the same sense of social excitement was absent from its online experience. This realization led the company to apply for a patent for what it called "enhancing online shopping atmosphere" on its websites. As Apple put it, "One drawback of online shopping is that the experience can feel sterile and isolating. Customers in such an environment may be less likely to have positive feelings about the online shopping experience, may be less inclined to engage in the online equivalent of window shopping (e.g., will not linger in front of a display), and may ultimately spend less money than their counterparts who shop in physical stores."[2]

Apple intended to reimagine the design of its websites to better inform visitors of areas where other online shoppers were active or gathering on its site. It could be a hot new product introduction, a new service offering or some other event. "For example," the patent read, "if an author has been invited to participate in a live chat hosted by the store, an icon of the book may appear in [a region] alerting customers (in all departments) that a special event is occurring." In essence, Apple sought to make its website feel more like a physical store.

What Apple knew then remains just as true today. There can be an indescribable vibe to a physical shopping experience. The dynamics created by real-world crowds feed into our innate fear of missing out on a good thing, and it's this flash of excitement that makes for memorable and addictive retail experiences.

We shop because it's physiological

Our brains love shopping. In fact, when it's good, retail is essentially a legalized form of crack. No joke. Our neurological response to a great shopping experience is virtually identical to the one produced by crack cocaine—because they're both reliable producers of a chemical called dopamine.

Dopamine is a neurotransmitter that controls our sense of pleasure, motivation, attention or action. Put more simply, dopamine is a reward chemical that moves through our brains when something gives us pleasure; take your pick—sex, drugs, rock 'n' roll—dopamine is involved. Neuroscientist Vaughan Bell once called dopamine "the Kim Kardashian of neurotransmitters" because it turns up in the popular press so often. Its celebrity status is a result of playing a central role in so many of our addictive behaviors. And yes, for many of us, shopping is addictive. The next time you're at an outlet mall, look at the faces of the people standing in the checkout lines. These are the faces of dopamine. Faces that Dr. Robert Sapolsky is all too familiar with.

Sapolsky is a professor of biology, neuroscience and neurosurgery at Stanford University. Among other things, he's known for his studies of dopamine production in the brains of monkeys, which provide a means of better understanding the causes and effects of the chemical on humans. The results of his experiments offer retailers an important hint as to how dopamine influences shopper behavior. In one experiment, monkeys were trained to complete a short task. Once completed, the monkey would receive a food treat. Each time a new session was about to begin, a small light would come on, prompting the monkey to begin the task. The monkey would then go to work. Each time the task was completed, a reward was dispensed.

Sapolsky's assumption was that dopamine levels in the monkeys' brains would be at their highest when they received the reward; however, that proved not to be the case. In fact, the dopamine level in the monkeys' brains rose immediately upon seeing the flashing light, which signaled that the opportunity to earn a reward was imminent. In other words, it was not the reward itself, but the *anticipation* of the reward that prompted the greatest release of dopamine to the brain.

And it gets even more interesting. Sapolsky also found that if the reward was granted 100 percent of the time after the monkeys performed the task, their dopamine levels remained average. But as soon as the odds of receiving a reward dropped to less than 100 percent, the monkeys' dopamine levels rose. In fact, by the time the odds of success changed to 50/50, their dopamine levels went through the roof! In other words, the guarantee of getting what we crave produces *less* dopamine than is the case when there's some risk of coming up empty-handed.

This explains many things. It explains gambling, dating, religion, drug addiction and employee incentive programs. It also tells us something important about shopping. A shopper's dopamine levels will be at their highest in *anticipation* of acquiring the thing they seek, and those levels will be even higher if there's a known risk of not getting it. This outcome also goes a long way toward explaining the enduring appeal of off-price stores, outlet malls and even rummage sales, where shoppers have to treasure-hunt for bargains in their size, color or style. The mere fact that they may or may not find what they like produces enhanced dopamine levels.

We can infer from this research that as massive marketplaces such as Amazon continue to expand their selections, thereby raising the odds of customers finding precisely what they want, they're inadvertently lowering the level of dopamine production associated with shopping on their sites. While the increased certainty of finding what we want on Amazon might appeal to the rational part of our brains, it makes for a dopamine-light experience, which ultimately will feel less satisfying. This spells opportunity for conventional retailers.

> "I spend all day thinking of shopping.
> I love the thrill of finding that wonderful,
> perfect thing, the feeling of your heart racing
> because it's so right." **MINDY GROSSMAN**

In fact, retailers such as Costco raise shopper dopamine levels through a well-plied strategy of stocking unique items, but doing so in very limited quantities. As a result, Costco shoppers become trained to operate with an innate fear of missing out, which, we know, raises dopamine levels and frequently compels them to buy more than they intended to. I often say that Costco is the only place I know where you can go in for pork chops and come out with a kayak. Blame dopamine!

So, as far as our brains are concerned, truly amazing retail walks a fine line between delivering consistency and dependability while also injecting the randomness of organic discovery and the fear of missing out. The subtle degree of chaos that we find in a physical shopping experience can, if engineered properly, add to the excitement of discovery. In other words, great shopping experiences are a sublime combination of predictability and chance.

Online to offline

These human elements of retail may well explain why a steady stream of online pure-play retailers are setting up physical stores. One by one, companies have been stepping out of the digital realm and manifesting in the strange physical reality we call stores. In fact, at least twenty online retailers have made the leap in just the past few years. These include startups such as Warby Parker, which in 2010 turned the optical market on its head with a unique online, virtual try-on business model. And Vancouver-based Indochino, an online maker of custom men's suits. And Everlane, a pure-play disruptor in men's and women's fashions. And even Amazon—yes Amazon, the company that spent the past twenty years putting bookstores out of business, is opening both bookstores and convenience stores!

So, if digital retailing is the only way forward, why are these brands spending hard-earned capital building physical stores? If real estate is a ball and chain dragging brands to the bottom of the retail ocean, why on earth are these companies investing in it? Why would they venture into what Marc Andreessen characterized as the hopeless abyss of untenable costs, productivity pitfalls and financial fucked-up-ed-ness?

For Warby Parker, the answer was simple: stores are an important means of building relationships with its customers. While the brand's original business plan was designed to preclude the need for brick and mortar entirely by offering customers the ability to do a home try-on, co-founder Neil Blumenthal found customers ultimately wanted a physical store. He explains:

Within 48 hours of launch, we were overwhelmed by demand and had to suspend the home trial program. And people would call up and say, 'Hey, can we come to your office and try on glasses?' And we would say, 'Uh, we are working out of my apartment.'

People would come in, and we would lay out the glasses on the dining room table. And we thought it was going to be a sub-optimal experience, but it ended up being a very special experience in that we could build relationships with our customers. They could try on all the glasses. We started to realize maybe there was a place for traditional bricks-and-mortar retail.[3]

Those early customer encounters in Blumenthal's apartment proved powerful enough to lead the brand to open thirty-five showrooms across the U.S. and Canada. He's quick to point out, however, that these are not at all typical optical stores. According to Blumenthal, "It's about how can we create special moments. When you walk into the store, most people are really surprised, because it doesn't look like any place they have ever been that sells eye glasses."[4]

Online custom suit maker Indochino also sees a future paved with bricks and mortar. The brand, founded in 2007, opened seven stores in 2014. By 2015, it had announced plans to open another 150 globally. Taking a page from the playbook of another successful online men's brand, Bonobos, the stores are not places that stock products but rather "showrooms" where men can get fitted and select styles and fabrics for their suits.

Even Everlane, the online fashion retailer that made its mark in 2011 by seemingly defying so many of the typical industry conventions such as the seasonality of collections, opted to launch its first permanent store in San Francisco's Mission

District in 2016. The store is aimed at providing a place for customers not only to explore and try on harder-to-fit items but also to work with well-trained Everlane stylists.

Given Amazon's notorious secrecy and labyrinthine strategies, we may never fully understand its initial motivation for opening stores. I did, however, meet up with several of its store development team at a conference I was speaking at and can confirm this much: Amazon's views on physical stores are anything but conventional and it's certainly not opening bookstores because it needs to sell more books. In fact, it's my firm belief that the "bookstores" are mere Trojan horses that allow Amazon to address far more critical underlying business opportunities.

First, each new Amazon store can act as an important mini-distribution hub for the consolidation, delivery and customer pickup of local orders, reducing its cost structure for last-mile delivery—which we know is paramount to Amazon's profitability. Consider a world where Amazon dots the landscape with small, efficient convenience and bookstores giving shoppers the ability to pick up almost anything they order on a next-day basis.

Second, and perhaps more importantly, these stores provide a live showcase for Amazon's digital devices, such as the Fire Tablet, Fire TV, Kindle ereaders, Echo digital assistants and Dash Buttons. Unlike Apple stores, which famously entreated customers to discover, touch and play with new devices, Amazon has had no such proprietary touch-and-play point in the market until now. As a result, the company hasn't been able to penetrate the market with its devices nearly as adeptly as Apple has—a lost opportunity considering that Amazon's devices are, in essence, the portals to the entire Amazon value proposition.

There is another reason that physical stores are important, and it's a reason I suspect the team at Amazon is all too aware of. Physical stores unquestionably catalyze online sales, simply by raising brand awareness in each given market. As David Gilboa, co-founder of Warby Parker, said, "We also see a halo effect where stores themselves become a great generator of awareness for our brand and drive a lot of traffic to our website, and accelerate our e-commerce sales."[5] Gilboa isn't alone in his observation. Indochino CEO Drew Green echoes a similar experience, saying, "Anytime we open a store in a city, we see awareness and sales in that city grow four times compared to what it was previously, as online-only."[6] I've also confirmed the same phenomenon with a number of large consumer brands. When they open a physical store, the result is very often an immediate jump in online sales. The math is physical stores equal more online sales.

Above all else, though, physical locations offer the ability to stage shopper experiences—experiences that are vital to unlocking the loyalty of a new and decidedly different generation of consumers.

Generation Ex(perience)

THEY'VE BEEN CALLED lazy, self-absorbed and entitled. They're largely disenfranchised with respect to the political system and feel that Establishment leaders are out of touch. They shun consumerism, home ownership and traditional values such as marriage and favor handmade things over mass-manufactured goods. They are idealists who believe their work should serve a higher purpose beyond financial gain and make many of their consumer decisions based on concern for the environment.

Who would you say I've just described?

If you said millennials, or Gen Y, you'd be wrong.

In fact, I was talking about their parents: the baby boomer generation. Forty years ago, these were the very words being used to sum up what at the time were a bunch of pot-smoking, peace-loving hippies. Yet, who would ever have imagined then that this same generation would go on to poke a hole in the ozone layer, turn Wall Street into a weapon of mass financial destruction and preside over more global conflict than any other generation in the planet's history?

If there's a lesson in this, it's that in seeking to sum up an entire generation in a few neat, tidy catchphrases and generalized behaviors, we not only risk getting them wrong, we risk losing them as customers. Yet many retailers today are doing both.

Millennials are those born between 1984 and 2004, and they are quite possibly one of the most overanalyzed and yet misunderstood generations in history. Some of this confusion, of course, is a consequence of timing and circumstance. Only a decade ago, marketers believed they had millennials pegged as the new power consumers with an insatiable appetite for luxury goods. This generation was spending at five hundred times the rate that their parents had at the same age, and retailers were gleefully rubbing their hands together in anticipation of this massive cohort leaning fully into their prime replacement-spending years. The party appeared to just be getting started. Then the music stopped when a speed bump called the longest recession in history happened, and the dream of "millennials gone wild" proved just that... a dream. Today, retailers are accusing millennials of being a bunch of disaffected paupers who eschew material belongings—*digital natives* who favor fast, disposable fashion and turn their backs on luxury brands; a generation that would rather spend what little money it has on experiences instead of products.

So, which is it? Are millennials the future of retail or the harbingers of its downfall? Are they power consumers or anticonsumers? It might be helpful to separate fact from fiction. First, the facts:

→ Millennials will account for one-third of total spending by 2020.[1] They are unquestionably a huge demographic cohort, and much of the retail economy will hinge on their participation in it.
→ They are graduating post-secondary institutions with debt. In the U.S., for example, 71 percent of graduates have debt

averaging approximately thirty thousand dollars.[2] This debt load, along with constrained employment opportunities, may be largely responsible for delaying other life events such as marriage, children and home ownership—all important consumer milestones that feed replacement spending.

→ In North America and many European countries, millennial incomes have lagged behind the national average. In the U.S., for example, those under thirty are now less well off than the retired.[3]

→ Fewer millennials own homes than those their age in previous generations, with a greater percentage renting or living with their parents for much longer.

→ They are more concentrated in major cities. In the U.S., for example, the growth of cities is now outpacing suburbs for the first time since the 1920s. This renewed urbanism has posed challenges for big-box retailers eager to reach this cohort with physical stores.

→ They are mobile first. In almost every developed market, millennials represent the highest mobile user segment, especially on smartphones.

→ They are innately social, spending above-average amounts of time on social networks such as Facebook, Instagram and Snapchat. They are also notoriously quick to change social networks as new ones come along.

These things are true and verifiable.

However, when it comes to retail I'm sure you've also heard that millennials have no need for, or interest in, physical shopping experiences. They are purported to be mobile animals who avoid trips to stores in favor of ordering *everything* from a smartphone. They are, to put it bluntly, the architects of physical retail's Armageddon. But, this, I'm afraid, is where the truth-train comes to a stop. There is not a shred of evidence that millennials don't enjoy physical stores. In fact, the exact opposite is true.

A 2016 U.K.-based study found that physical stores are *most* valued by younger consumers, noting: "The age groups most attached to stores are 16–24 and 25–34 year olds. Their use of online pure-play retailers is also notably low. This not only reinforces the importance of physical stores today, but also indicates their likely future importance."[4]

Another extensive study by research firm Accenture echoed similar results, stating, "Many members of the digital generation actually prefer visiting stores to shopping online. What's more, our research findings in the United States were reflected in the other countries where we surveyed as well. Echoing countless generations of canny shoppers, one Millennial told us, 'You want to touch it; you want to smell it; you want to pick it up.'"[5]

Research within specific categories of merchandise suggests that 91 percent of millennials prefer to shop in physical drugstores versus online alternatives, 68 percent prefer physical electronics stores, 84 percent prefer shopping in physical department stores and 83 percent prefer shopping in physical discount and mass retailers.[6]

Yet another study found that nearly half of millennials value the experience they have with a brand more than the product itself. This number compared to only 22 percent of baby boomers. Forty-eight percent of millennials feel that the experience they have with a brand is the greatest predicator of loyalty, compared with 17 percent of boomers who feel the same.[7]

Make no mistake. Millennials are big fans of physical experiences. And if you need any more evidence of this affinity for the physical, look no further than the music industry, where live events have reached unprecedented popularity. For example, in July of 2015 the Coachella Valley Music and Arts Festival hit a milestone when sales exceeded $84.25 million with 198,000 tickets sold—a record for the event, which has been in existence since 1999. Attendance records are nothing new for Coachella; it has beaten its own benchmarks consecutively in each of the past four years. Coachella's success isn't unique, either. Lollapalooza, The Governors Ball and Bonnaroo have all enjoyed similar exponential growth.

So, why is this happening? In an age when nearly free music is as ubiquitous as running water, why do 198,000 people camp at a three-day music festival in a desert valley in southern California? There may be many reasons, but at the heart is the promise of a kinetic experience. They go not only to hear music but to feel it and, in a way, become one with it. They go to be part of a living social thing—to soak up its energy. In a world where almost every aspect of our lives has been somehow digitalized, experiences that engage our bodies, our senses and our souls are at a premium.

Digital is what we've become and yet visceral is what we are... it's what we crave. Our need to detach from the Internet and escape to reality, if only for a while, is powerful and will continue to grow as we become increasingly chained to technology.

It's not them... it's us

So, if we're honest about it, the problem isn't that millennials dislike physical stores; it's that most store experiences suck. I'm not saying this lightly or for effect. I mean it sincerely. Most stores we visit are devoid of any theater, excitement or aesthetic delight, much less any sort of engaging physical experience. The vast majority of retail stores are havens of humdrum and bastions of boredom!

Don't take my word for it; think of your own experiences. When was the last time you had a jaw-dropping experience in a mall, department store or shop? Honestly, when was the last time you walked right out of a retail store and told a friend or family member about it because you were so excited about what you'd just experienced?

We have to face it sooner or later: most retail stores are about as fun and enthralling as a traffic jam! And for a generation of consumers that has been exposed to unprecedented levels of digital stimuli their entire lives, most of the stores they walk into must feel simply mind-numbing. There's nothing inspiring about a Home Depot; there's nothing fun about a Walmart. Take the logo off a Macy's store and it could be a JCPenney. Do the same at JCPenney and you may as well be standing in a Lord & Taylor or a Hudson's Bay store. Different logo, same boredom! To be fair, these retailers are by no means the only offenders. This condition repeats itself in thousands of malls, main streets and stores around the world. Even the palatial flagships in cities such as Hong Kong, London, Singapore, New York and L.A. all form the same soup of sameness once you get over the superficial glitz.

It's an epidemic that has even turned some retailers to the desperate act of fabricating faux excitement. My wife and I were in a department store in Florida not long ago when all of a sudden we heard a racket coming from somewhere nearby. We could hear what sounded like horns blowing and drums beating but we couldn't make out exactly what was going on. Eventually a parade of store staff half-heartedly playing musical instruments rounded the corner and began to make its way up the aisle toward us. It was an oddly somber sight, like a conga line en route to the gallows. We asked a salesperson what was happening, and he told us that store management made the employees parade around the store several times a day to "create a buzz." By the look on his face, we didn't have to ask how he and his colleagues felt about it.

Other retailers have attempted to make their store environments relevant by jumping—often without any sort of cohesive plan—into technology. The battle cry has been to create "digital experiences," which in itself is problematic for a few reasons:

→ Too many retailers are simply bolting technology onto what is most often a mediocre customer experience instead of reimagining the customer experience entirely and then, where it makes sense, using technology to enable or enhance it.

→ They're making a huge assumption that consumers are craving more engagement with technology than they already have each day. In a world where we're looking at our phones 220 times a day, a physical store shouldn't simply be a place to go and look at it for the 221st time. A store needs to be a place where magic happens and, sometimes, that magic might involve technology but it needn't have to.

→ Many assume that the way to a millennial's heart is through a smartphone or some other technology, but as we now know, this isn't necessarily the case. Yes, millennials are mobile and connected, but they're also extremely physical beings. In fact, they are more experientially oriented than older generations.

A physical store should celebrate its physicality, allowing one to touch, try, feel and experience products in a visceral way. It's not about watching a golf video in a sporting goods store. It's swinging a golf club. It's not about standing in the middle of a dusty warehouse speaking to a chatbot about product needs. It's relating with an enthusiastic and delightfully human product expert who is empowered with technology that makes them even more expert. It's not about using virtual reality to escape the boredom of the store. It's using a remarkable store to escape reality—to enter a different world—just for a while.

Technology can and should be used to enable experiences wherever possible, but we must never lose sight of the fact that consumers crave physical experiences. We have an almost primordial need to interact, to touch, to handle the objects we gather before we buy them, and to do so in active, vibrant, social spaces. The convenience technology offers can never entirely subjugate the humanity at the core of why we shop.

So, finding the critical balance between the physical and the digital begins with skillful and thoughtful experiential design. Searching for experiential inflection points where shoppers can be physically engaged and immersed is key. Technology can be the spark that brings remarkable store experiences to life or it can be the connective tissue between the moments along the path to purchase, but retailers must never lose sight of the intrinsic physicality and joyfully kinetic nature of live retail.

In a way, every store needs to be a small Coachella experience—an experience that engages all five senses and remains with shoppers long after they've left the store. An experience they feel in every cell.

All indicators suggest that millennials are desperate for outstanding live shopping opportunities. They're dying to discover retailers that can engage them with amazing products with which they can play, learn, experiment and have a remarkable time doing so. They long for moments that they can't replicate at home or on a mobile device. They want retailers that can deliver mind-boggling physical shopping. Frankly, regardless of age, that's what we've *all* been waiting for.

So, what's standing in the way? If consumers want exciting, engaging and remarkable experiences and retailers are aware that's what they want, then why aren't brands stepping up to the challenge and delivering those experiences in their stores? It's certainly not that retail executives aren't well intentioned, capable or smart. It's not that there isn't a sense of urgency to change; trust me, there is. It's not that consumers aren't open to the transformation of retail. They are!

What's holding retail back is actually much, much deeper, and if we're ever going to transform the retail experience, we're going to need to confront it and correct it sooner or later. The intrinsic problem is that the core metrics used to judge the productivity of a retail store—the very measures by which success in this industry is currently defined—are conspiring against the vital evolution of customer experiences. Any attempts by retail executives to be creative, innovative, daring or disruptive ultimately get measured using the most conventional and passionless yardstick of them all—*sales per square foot.*

In essence, we're attempting to create retail poetry by using algebra. And it just doesn't work.

The economics of boredom

Consider that in the past two hundred years we've seen innovation that has ranged from the lightbulb to nanotechnology, and yet the way we measure retail success hasn't fundamentally changed since Bloomingdale's opened its doors in 1872! Sales per square foot, sales per employee, comparable store growth and inventory turns—we've used the same metrics since before the advent of penicillin. How is this even possible?

Even more worrisome is that these metrics are the highlighted figures in shareholder reports—the ones executives, analysts and investors zero in on first. They're the numbers that prompt activist shareholders to insist that brands close the very stores that give them the essential brand presence they require to drive sales across channels. They're the numbers that inhibit innovation, creativity and courage. These are the numbers that make smart people do dumb things.

To understand what I mean, put yourself in the shoes of a category buyer for Macy's. In your role, what is the number one criterion that you, as the buyer, would place above all else when deciding which products to bring into your stores? I suspect you said "sales." And that's exactly right. Sales per square foot is the metric that almost every buyer obsesses over. Because according to orthodox retail thinking, unless a product will sell in significant volume, the square footage it occupies simply can't be justified. In fact, without strong square-foot sales performance, buyers lose square footage to other departments. And eventually they lose their jobs to other buyers.

Retail, today, lives and dies by square-foot sales. And it is for that single reason that a plethora of unique, fun, fashionable and fascinating products, concepts and innovations will likely never see the light of day on a major chain's sales floor. This one metric throws cold water on any flame of creativity.

What buyer is going to risk their job to fill a large amount of floor space with products that are unlikely to sell in large quantity—even if those products might add exponentially to overall shopper enjoyment or enhance their sense of discovery? What buyer will gamble on taking space from products and giving it to cool experiences—even if those experiences might wildly delight their shoppers? The reality is, while almost every business talks about creating customer delight, very few buyers get their bonuses based on delivering it. How whack is that? And the really awful part is that the worse sales become, the more entrenched the obsession with per-square-foot productivity becomes, creating a downward spiral toward even more bland and boring stores and even lower sales.

Now, repeat the Macy's buyer's mandate across the thousands and thousands of retail buyers around the world, each of whom is following the same guiding metric, and soon every store in the mall begins to look the same. Every mall looks exactly like the next. And before you know it, you have a pandemic of boredom, with every store attempting to sell the same safe-bet products, designs and brands as the last; every one of them is terrified to use its floor space for unique or exciting experiences, entertainment or demonstrations, and paralyzed to venture out on a limb to delight its customers.

As a shopper, any hope of discovering something new, exciting and unexpected at your local department store has evaporated because there isn't a buyer in the country who will bet on any product that might really catch you by surprise. No one is willing to yield inventory space to experience.

So, it's not that consumers are killing retail. *Retailers* are killing retail and consumers are just innocent eyewitnesses to the crime. As long as retailers insist on maintaining their myopic focus on sales per square foot, stores will suffer, shoppers will get shortchanged and retailers will compound their difficulties.

It's a problem now made all the more profound because consumer expectations of variety, selection and discovery are being pervasively shaped by the endless sea of unique products we can find online. Unlike physical stores that have to commit to minimum inventories, Amazon can be the Noah's Ark of retail, stocking two of everything on Earth if it wishes. Etsy doesn't even have to stock a single product in order to offer almost anything you can imagine! Alibaba has thousands of merchants selling everything under the sun. Consequently, online is where you're likely to spot the next cool new product—*not in a store*. And this is a huge, glaring existential problem for retailers.

And so, as we move into the future, something has to give. Something has to break this cycle of boredom in physical stores. And the road to salvation begins with expanding our view of how success in a physical store can be measured above and beyond per-square-foot sales. We need to completely reinvent the purpose of a physical store and the means by which we measure its success.

And this is where you may want to drop another red pill. Because what I'm really saying is that the purpose of a physical retail store can no longer be to sell products.

The Shopping Space
of the Future

WITHIN A DECADE, sensor-driven replenishment, predictive analytic technology, immersive digital shopping experiences, subscription programs and a myriad of other connected shopping
options—many of which we can't yet even conceive of—will very
effectively cater to our day-to-day product needs. We will never
again wonder if we have milk in the fridge or detergent in the
laundry room. We will order furniture and fashion online with
implicit confidence because haptic technologies will give us the
ability to touch and feel what we buy before we buy. Apparel-fit-
ting algorithms infused with big data analytics will ensure the
items we purchase are almost always ideally suited to both our
bodies and our tastes. Using virtual or augmented reality technology in our home or office to shop and connect with product
experts will be as common in ten years as shopping in a physical store is today. And ultra-rapid and free delivery via a range
of transport modes will put any product on our doorstep in
minutes.

Save for a very few particular kinds of products, we will have absolutely no need to visit physical stores simply to look at products, as we do today. It's that simple. Instead, the physical shopping space will become a medium to distribute the most powerful, joyful and emotionally galvanizing experiences possible. These *physical media* experiences will be aimed at accomplishing three things:

→ conveying clear and engaging brand stories through physical engagement and multiple sensory inputs
→ offering opportunities for immersive and kinetic product experiences
→ acting as the interactive gateway to the entire brand ecosystem of products, services and purchase alternatives

Notice I didn't mention anything about selling products. This, of course, is not to suggest that the retail space of the future won't sell products—but that the sale of those products from within the four walls of the store will cease to be a priority. Instead, the goal of the store will be to create experiences so powerful that they catalyze sales across all available purchase points and channels.

Renowned retail shopping center developer Allan Zeman once said that it was time to reverse the design standard in malls, which have traditionally been 70 percent retail and 30 percent entertainment. The shopping center, he said, must be a place for entertainment first and retail second. Without a heavy emphasis on entertainment, Zeman maintained, people will have little reason to go to the mall at all. Similarly, I'm suggesting to you that in order to be viable in the future, retailers must apply this same approach to how they plan, design, build and operate their physical spaces: experiences first and foremost and products second.

I realize that this vision of the future is hard to square up with retail as we know it today. In the current era, retailers spend a disproportionate amount of their time busying themselves with products. They buy them, inventory them, move them from place to place, merchandise and itemize them. They mark them up, mark them down, sell them, accept them back as returns and then physically count every damn one of them at least once a year. It's to the point that in most retail companies, so many resources go to the movement and maintenance of product that customer experience becomes an afterthought, a mere garnish.

But in the retail space of the future, the most important product will be the experiences it offers shoppers. And the most successful retailers of tomorrow will obsess over the design, execution and measurement of experiences. In a world of unabated product proliferation, where just about any product can be reverse-engineered within days or weeks, experiences represent the last remaining fortress of differentiation and consumer value a retailer will have. Anyone can knock off your product—that's easy. But recreating the unique alchemy of people, place, purpose and production that forms a wicked brand experience is infinitely more difficult, if not impossible, to copy. Consider how long other retailers have unsuccessfully been trying to replicate the Apple experience; and product has little to do with it. The truth is, Apple could sell shoes, groceries or pet food and its stores would likely be just as cool.

Moving the emphasis away from product distribution and toward the delivery of a physical media experience will change the very nature of how stores are conceived, located, designed, staffed, managed and measured.

"The future is already here—it's just not evenly distributed." **WILLIAM GIBSON**

Individual listening rooms where customers can enjoy their
favorite music as it fills the space in the New York City Sonos store.

I'm very often asked which retailers today are executing against this "store as media" future, and while there is no single retailer that I believe embodies the vision completely, there are a number that, to varying degrees, are evolving toward the concept. In other words, this shopping space of the future actually exists today, just not all in one place. But look closely enough and you'll see fragments of the future of retail scattered ever so finely throughout the market already. A small number of visionary entrepreneurs, brands and executives are out there right now poking at the retail universe to see what lies beyond and thumbing their noses at the rules the rest of the industry haplessly abides by.

So, what will the store of the future look, act and sound like? In my opinion it looks *more or less* like this:

Less distribution of products, more distribution of experiences

The shopping spaces of the future will not exist merely to facilitate the distribution of products; as consumers, we will no longer need them for that. In the future, trips to the store simply to pick up items that can be ordered and delivered almost instantly to your door will become the exception. The new purpose and intent of the shopping space will be to distribute *experiences with* those products. We will not go to a store to look at sporting goods but to try them. We won't drive five miles to pick up a pair of running shoes. We'll visit a shopping space to learn which shoe is ideal for the way we run. We won't venture to the grocery store to haul home a turkey. We will visit a retail space to learn how to properly cook one. We will travel to a shopping space to learn, play, experiment and experience in a way that is simply not possible from home—with or without technology.

Listen up

When Sonos founder and CEO John MacFarlane came up with the idea of streaming music to wireless speakers in the early 2000s, it was amazingly visionary. Today the market is brimming with competitive brands of speakers. Although Sonos speakers are awesome (full disclosure: my home is full of them), they're no longer novel or unique. That's prompted Sonos to reimagine how its speakers get sold.

When Sonos asked its customers where they were first exposed to its line of wireless speakers, many said in the comfort of a friend's home. With that insight in hand, Sonos built its first physical space in New York City with the aim of providing shoppers that same sense of place and comfort.

The brand's new 4,200-square-foot retail space showcases enclosed listening rooms furnished like a stylish friend's apartment. Each room is perfectly acoustically tuned, soundproofed and beautifully designed by a well-known interior designer. And each space is outfitted with a unique combination of speakers and equipment, which allows shoppers to move from room to room to have different listening experiences and to learn about different products and configurations in a fully experiential way. Acoustic nirvana.

The design of the space is rounded out with unique pieces of custom artwork that pay tribute to music, sound and technology and also features open lounge spaces where Sonos' visitors can just hang and chill out. According to Dmitri Siegel, Sonos' vice president of global brand and executive creative director, "The whole store experience is based on the idea of being in a really comfortable and inspiring environment, listening to music you love, but hearing it in a way you never have before."[1]

Of course, it would have been much easier and less costly for Sonos to do what most other electronics brands do—simply build its product into a very practical and basic store design and fill the store floor with loads of inventory. Instead, the Sonos space seeks to wrap the product up in an unforgettable, one-of-a-kind listening experience. Sonos doesn't want you to just see the product with your eyes or hear it with your ears; it wants you to feel it with every nerve ending in your body.

What Sonos understands is that the world has no need for another electronics store. It needs beautiful spaces where people can gather to celebrate the unique sensorial joy of listening to music.

Less a store, more a story

Very few brands can lay claim to the creation of more remarkable and memorable guest experiences than Disney, which anyone who has been to a Disney theme park will attest to. It is, by most accounts, the master at creating magical moments in people's lives. It's no surprise, then, that retailers and brands from across the globe travel to Disney each year to learn how it does what it does—create experiences—so well.

Turns out, it all begins with a story.

Legendary Disney theme park designer John Hench once said, "Story is the essential organizing principle behind the design of the Disney theme parks." For Hench and his team, a successful theme park was a zeitgeist of cast, costumes, set design, technology and attractions centered on a compelling narrative. "We transform a space into a story space," he said. "Every element must work together to create an identity that supports the story of that place."[2]

What Hench recognized all those years ago—and what smart retailers are coming to recognize now—is that no amount of store design, technology, product or merchandising can replace the essential bedrock of a powerful brand story. It's not that these other things don't matter; of course they do. But without a cohesive and powerful story that people care about, these other elements will be largely ineffective. All icing... no cake.

Great retailers of the future will build their shopping spaces less as stores and more as remarkable places that put story at the nucleus of the shopping experience. For example, every attribute of the first Apple store—including store design, merchandising, staffing, service methodology and in-store technology—supported the brand story "Think Different" and the battle cry of defying the status quo. The store was, in every sense, unique compared to any computer store that came before it. As such, it was a living, breathing articulation of Apple's brand story.

Every retailer, no matter what they sell, must instill this same element of story into their shopping spaces. But let me be clear, what I am suggesting is not that your retail space become a stuffy museum for your brand. It's not a place where your story is told in a passive way through a few signs, screens or pictures hung on a wall. Story is not something that we put in front of shoppers for them to reflexively gaze at. It's something we draw them into.

I'm also not suggesting here that every brand story need be told in the same high-touch manner or with lofty in-store aesthetics. The fact is, a dollar store can have just as powerful and engaging a brand story as a luxury apparel store, if it's well designed and articulated.

Ultimately, shoppers should become active participants in your brand story. After all, story is what we see, hear, taste, touch and engage with. It's the people we talk with and the feeling we take home with us. Story helps you bring the same feeling into your retail space that you might find in Disney's Magic Kingdom. It's that feeling of entering a completely different world.

Adventure story

At the grand opening of their first Globetrotter equipment store in Hamburg in 1979, Klaus Denart and Peter Lechhart served their customers live mealworms. This might not sound like a recipe for retail success, but for Denhart, an avid global adventurer who had paddled the Nile, climbed mountains and traversed jungles, and Lechhart, his friend and a professional adventure guide, it was a most fitting first chapter in the retail story of their mutual passion for serious outdoor adventure.

From this eccentric beginning, Globetrotter has grown into a €200 million per year business as Europe's largest independent retailer of outdoor gear, with a dozen locations across Germany. Mealworms were just one of the immersive experiences Denhart and Lechart had in store for customers as they related their unique story through the experiences that shoppers could have with them rather than the products they could buy.

Today, Globetrotter's retail spaces are like amusement parks for outdoorspeople, featuring such elements as high-altitude chambers where climbers can prepare themselves for major ascents; a 220,000-liter scuba diving, canoeing and sailing pool where shoppers can dive, paddle and sail; a glass climbing tunnel where enthusiasts and novices alike can try out gear; an arctic chamber to test cold-weather equipment and clothing; and even a storm chamber to test waterproof clothing in simulated tsunami-type conditions.

Each section of the store provides opportunities to actually try products. For example, the shoe department offers terrain runs that simulate a variety of hiking surfaces. Even the toilets in the store are designed to simulate those found in ships and trains and feature screens that show exotic scenery passing by. If that weren't enough, their stores offer immunization clinics for malaria and yellow fever among other diseases, and onsite travel agents who can help you book your next adventure. Best of all, visitors can even arrange to camp in the store overnight to test out tents and other gear.

A casual Google search will turn up significantly more rave TripAdvisor reviews of Globetrotter than it will posts from Globetrotter itself. The experience that its retail outlets provide has become a tremendously valuable source of earned media.

Every aspect of Globetrotter's retail spaces articulates a deep and authentic story of the love of adventure and passion for the outdoors. It's not only a story that confirms to avid outdoorspeople that they've come to the right place, but as reviews point out, it's also a story that is transformational, turning even casual shoppers into outdoor enthusiasts. Globetrotter is a living, breathing stage production of outdoor adventure, and every customer who enters its stores can become an actor on that stage.

Less take, more make

Twenty years from now, you will marvel at the idea that you went to a store to fill a basket with products, emptied the contents of that basket onto a conveyor, loaded the items back into the basket, emptied the goods from your basket into your car, unloaded the items from the car and then finally loaded your purchases into your home. All that loading and unloading will seem like insanity. Luckily, most of the commodity products we need on a regular basis will simply arrive as we need them, based on our consumption patterns.

Therefore, the retail space of the future will not be a place we go to simply *take* something home. It will, more often than not, be a place we go to *make* something. No longer merely passive pack mules, shoppers will take an active role in customizing and personalizing the items they're interested in.

If we are indeed embarking on a world where I can co-design my own new automobile and then watch while it's 3D printed before my very eyes, it stands to reason that we're going to increasingly want a hand in tailoring more of the things we purchase to our unique needs and specifications.

Therefore, our willingness to log out of Amazon, get off the sofa and head to a store will be driven by our interest in taking an active role in the conception of our unique product. The experience of engaging with the process, the place and the people who work there will be as valuable to us as the product itself.

Our role as consumers will steadily evolve from product transportation to product co-creation. The retail space will be our workshop!

Heeling properties

One store that's incorporating this notion today is Tanya Heath Paris, a footwear boutique specializing in shoes that offer interchangeable and customizable heels. When she dreamed up the idea for her product, Heath was a Canadian expat working in Paris as a management consultant and teaching a course in disruptive innovation at one of France's leading engineering

Paris-based Tanya Heath stores allow shoppers to fully customize
their choice of footwear, including interchangeable heels.

schools. She spent the next two and a half years collaborating
with fourteen engineers to design a shoe on which various heel
heights and styles could be easily swapped out. Today, Tanya
Heath Paris operates fourteen stores worldwide. In addition
to offering a wide variety of off-the-rack heels, the store also
employs in-store designers who can assist customers in creating
fully customized heels to match a specific piece of clothing or
accessory.

Recognizing this trend toward customization, U.S. retailer
Nordstrom recently took an equity stake in a similar customized
footwear startup called Shoes of Prey. Like Tanya Heath Paris,
Shoes of Prey allows shoppers to customize the design of their
shoes, including the style, materials and heel height. Nordstrom
has introduced Shoes of Prey boutiques in six of its U.S. locations.

The ability for customers to inject their own creativity and
personality into a product not only builds greater attachment to
that product but also results in a higher level of satisfaction with

the retailer. According to one study, shoppers are willing, on average, to pay 20 percent more for customized goods and "gave companies a 50 percent higher net promoter score—a standard way of measuring customer loyalty—than customers who bought regular products from the same manufacturer."[3]

The retail space of the future, therefore, will be much more a workshop and design studio than the old-fashioned store we live with today.

Less static, more immersive

Inside of a decade, our ability to find, view and learn about products in a very real-feeling way will be completely transformed by immersive technologies, including virtual and augmented reality. As a result, our need, as shoppers, to physically travel to a store merely to view items will become almost nonexistent.

The static, dusty warehouses of product we find in big-box retailers of today will be all but eradicated. A Home Depot store as it exists now will eventually become a "dark store" whose sole purpose is to act as a shipping and pickup point for online orders. We will have no use for stores like this going forward. They will be anachronisms of an age of retail long passed.

Understanding that mediocre product interactions and experiences will no longer suffice, the shopping space of the future will take product trial, inspiration and education to an entirely new level, allowing shoppers to use, try and experiment with products in creative and entertaining ways. Don't be surprised to see bedding stores open spa-like spaces where shoppers can go for pampering and a good night's sleep on the mattress of their choice. Look for car dealerships to use their lots to house test tracks where buyers can test-drive vehicles instead of reserving that space for redundant inventory. Watch for outdoors stores to rely more on remote pop-up locations where climbers, hikers and other outdoor enthusiasts gather naturally, allowing them to try new gear in real-world conditions. Retailers across all categories will have to find unique and valuable ways to physicalize their shopping experience.

Bring your bathing suit

Pirch was founded in 2009 by Jim Stuart and Jeffery Sears, friends who found themselves working on separate home improvement projects but were equally dismayed at the level of indifference and lack of shopping experience available at big-box home improvement centers.

"Jim was building his dream house," says Laith Murad, Pirch's chief marketing officer. "He had retired, sold his company and had painted this romantic vision of his dream house, only to get disinterest, dissatisfaction and a kind of disheartening process" at big-box home improvement stores.[4] Store staff, he found, were more interested in selling what they had in stock rather than what was truly needed to suit his lifestyle. This, coupled with the fact that it was impossible to try any of the products, such as appliances, made for many a disappointing experience.

It proved to be so dismal, in fact, that Sears and Stuart wondered if shopping for home improvement projects could be done very differently. What if you could hear the sound the buttons on an appliance make when you push them? Or feel the water running from a tap? What if you could see the flame on the stove and maybe even cook with it before deciding to buy it? Surely, they believed, it would be a better shopping experience.

With that idea in mind, they launched Pirch.

Today, Pirch operates nine stores, with more on the horizon. Each store specializes in kitchen, bath and outdoor products. At approximately thirty thousand square feet in size, each store

Pirch kitchen, bath and outdoor stores feature
fully animated showrooms in which all the products
are working and ready for shoppers to try.
MARK STEELE

is a completely immersive shopping experience. You can cook alongside a professional chef; you can test appliances—many with prices akin to those of luxury cars. You can even take a shower—yes, take a shower—provided you bring a bathing suit, which Murad assures me several customers per week actually do! "How do you pick a showerhead if you don't know how it works?" he asks matter-of-factly. "People want to play, touch and feel."

Staff at Pirch come from all backgrounds and walks of life. The company places less emphasis on product knowledge and much more on personality. Product, Murad says, can be taught, but the right mindset for delighting customers is key. "Retail can be fun when you have the right culture, and the right theater and experience," he adds. "That's really different than saying, 'For every square foot, how do I make sure that every dollar is accounted for?' That's not who we are."[5]

A professional chef prepares for a
demonstration inside a Pirch showroom.
MARK STEELE

Who they are seems to be working. In fact, Pirch stores deliver a stupefying three thousand dollars per square foot in sales on average, placing them ahead of a pantheon of industry leaders including Apple and Tiffany & Co.

So how does a store that professes not to care about sales generate such incredible sales numbers? By building a culture that single-mindedly delivers great customer experiences.

Murad tells me that the challenge facing Pirch was not simply to sell products, but "in a cynical world, [to] create a culture of empathy and authenticity." It's an ethos that strives to make the time spent in a Pirch store thoroughly delightful and memorable.

Far from esoteric, this notion of customer enjoyment is very much tied to the company's Elements of Joy Manifesto: a set of guiding principles every employee is asked to model their behavior against. Unlike most dusty corporate employee handbooks, however, the Elements of Joy fit on a single sheet of paper and include phrases such as *Be real* and *Tomorrow is promised to no one* and *Make time for family. In the end, they are everything.*

The philosophy at Pirch is that if its employees can achieve true happiness in their work and in their lives, they'll be more likely to share that happiness with every customer who comes to the store. Co-founder Sears summed it up in an interview with *Fortune* magazine saying, "Our job is to make every guest feel like their time in our store is the best part of their day, whether or not they buy anything."[6]

When I ask Murad how all that kumbaya actually gets measured, he assures me that it's not all about hugs and good feelings. Apart from sales and other financial metrics, he says the company's "net promoter score" (the number of people who would recommend the experience to a friend or family member) is key. "Even Yelp reviews," he says, are looked at closely, quickly adding that Pirch's Yelp scores exceed those of Four Seasons Hotels in every city the brand operates in, revealing yet another important aspect of the company's competitive mindset. For Pirch, the competition isn't Home Depot or Lowe's. The real competition is any other truly remarkable experience in the marketplace, regardless of category.

Less cash and carry, more community

Stores as we know them today are a gathering place for products—prettied-up warehouses, if you will. But as our ability to buy seamlessly across channels and technologies improves, physical shopping spaces will need to be better designed as gathering places for people.

As Angela Ahrendts, Apple's senior vice president of retail, recently put it while describing the Apple store of the future, "We don't really need to open more stores, but we need to open incredible places that almost behave like a town square, like a gathering place."[7]

The store of tomorrow will become a place that celebrates the activities and lifestyles associated with a range of products. We will go to stores to interact with others who share our passions. Product acquisition may happen within the four walls of the store or it may take place later, across an ecosystem of purchase alternatives; it won't matter either way. What will matter is that experiences and interactions in these remarkable spaces will act as the catalysts for a powerful relationship between a customer and a brand and forge a deep sense of customer community.

3,000 square feet of nothing!

A recipe for bankruptcy. That's how some hard-core retail executives today would surely look at the three thousand square feet of empty space on the third floor of Jennifer Bandier's Manhattan retail location. For Bandier, however, the vacuous space is anything but unproductive. It's three thousand square feet of pure, immersive, experiential magic and the ultimate expression of her brand. Bandier is the founder of the Manhattan-based yoga and fitness apparel store by the same name, a store that's managing to stand out in an increasingly crowded athleisure category, or "active fashion" as she prefers to call it.

To complement her small physical store, Bandier added a large yoga and fitness studio. Aptly dubbed Studio B, the space offers twenty-five different classes per week with a notable lineup of celebrity instructors. "Our classes are not free," Bandier says, "but that's really because we wanted to offer the best of the best."[8] According to Bandier, in the three months following the opening of the studio, foot traffic to the store doubled.

The chain now has five stores and sales that Bandier said appear to be on track to top $20 million, including sales online.

Bandier's Studio B, where customers can enjoy classes with celebrity trainers.

She has further plans to create a juice bar and an album listening space on the second floor. A former music manager, Bandier points out that music and fitness are almost inseparable. As if to drive the point home, a massive in-store sign calls out, "fashion, fitness, music." Beyond the classes it offers, Bandier is also a gathering point, often hosting events and panel discussions on topics of interest to its community of customers.

The main floor of the space includes a small, more traditional-looking store space, with a well-curated assortment of products—a nod to conventional retail. But far from traditional, Bandier points to a new era when the retail space transcends its historic commercial boundaries and becomes a source of entertainment and leisure—a place where the most important product being sold is the experience of coming together with like-minded enthusiasts.

The ground floor retail portion of Bandier's
Fifth Avenue location in New York City.

Bandier and brands like it are a call-out to all retailers that the shopping space of the future will be more a gathering point for communities of interest. Rather than simply being a destination for immediate commercial transactions, the retail space will become the center of social transformation: a place to commune with others who share our passion.

Fewer conversions, more converts

Given that we're moving toward a future state where the vast majority of purchases will become digital, the role of a retail shopping space will no longer be to convert shoppers into buyers within its four walls. *Conversion*, once a key metric, will be of little importance to the retailer of the future.

I say this for two reasons. First, even today transactions tell us very little about the qualitative value of the shopper experience. The mere fact that I bought something says little about my experience in the store. Second, even though I left the retail space empty-handed, we can no longer assume that my experience was negative or won't culminate in a digital purchase later. Transactions, in fact, only represent a portion of the value generated by a store. Until recently, though, this metric has been all we've had to evaluate store performance by, apart from anecdotal observations from staff.

The retailers of the future, however, will treat each interaction in their shopping space as the experiential gateway for customers to reach the entire brand ecosystem of products, purchase methods and services. To do this, they will use a range of offline analytic tools to develop a fuller picture of customer engagement levels in their spaces.

But how can brands begin to quantify the value of creating these sorts of transformational engagements? The first value comes in the indirect return on customer experience to the brand. For example, according to Apple CEO Tim Cook, Apple stores were visited by at least 1 million shoppers each day in 2015, or 365 million visitors that year. Each of those visits is not only a potential sale, but also an important consumer brand impression.

I suspect that Apple has done the math on the impact to the brand of 365 million potentially positive consumer impressions generated by its stores and what those impressions would cost if they were sought through conventional media on the open market. But here's the thing: unlike a fleeting ad or commercial, a store experience is a tremendously more engaged impression. And best of all, the costs associated with creating remarkable shopper impressions aren't incremental to the business like an ad campaign would be—they're already paid for! The store, the people and the products are already there.

There's also the compounding effect of consumers sharing those experiences with others. One recent study of ten thousand shoppers indicated that a full 56 percent had shared positive experiences with others.[9] And of course, those experiences are not simply being shared conversationally, as they have been in the past. They're reaching a much wider audience through a variety of social media channels.

The second value generated is the more direct financial impact on brands that excel at customer experience. According to a study by Forrester, a stock portfolio of leading companies in their Customer Experience Index had a cumulative performance gain of 43 percent over six years compared with an average of 14.5 percent for the S&P 500. Customer Experience Index laggards during the same period of time, however, saw a drop of 33.9 percent![10]

The third return on customer experience is, of course, the direct sales impacts that result during and downstream of remarkable in-store experiences, many of which may come days, weeks or even months later. Research shows that companies that outperform in customer experience generate a dramatic increase in revenues.[11] For the average company with revenues of a billion dollars, for example, the incremental customer experience revenue lifts were

→ $382.3 million for a fast-food restaurant.
→ $343.7 million for a retailer.
→ $343.6 million for a grocery chain.

The retailer of the future will ensure that means are in place to better connect shopper experiences in the retail space to the downstream purchases those experiences catalyze. In short, the role of the shopping space of the future will not be to convert shoppers into buyers; it will be to turn shoppers into fanatical, lifelong converts and advocates for the brand.

The merchant of Venice Beach

While traveling in Argentina in 2006, Blake Mycoskie was stunned and saddened at the sight of so many impoverished children who had to go without shoes, exposing them to a variety of potential illnesses. He was moved enough by the experience to create TOMS, a "one-for-one" business model in which for every pair of shoes sold, the company donates a pair of shoes to a child in need. Needless to say, TOMS had more than its fair share of skeptics questioning both the viability of the model and its true charitable impact. That was ten years ago, and Mycoskie's obvious success seems to have quelled many of the naysayers.

Seven years after embarking on his unconventional approach to selling shoes, Mycoskie decided to open an equally unusual retail space in Venice Beach, California—a space that can only be described as a super-cool community hangout masquerading as a retail space. The store features an espresso bar, plenty of relaxed lounge seating and comfortable outdoor spaces where people bring their dogs.

For a brand that began as a wholesaler and online retailer, the move to build a store was significant in terms of physically defining the TOMS brand. Mycoskie described his vision for the space: "We're going to give free Wi-Fi in a beautiful space on an incredible street. People are going hang out here all day and they're not going to buy anything."[12]

Some friends and colleagues warned that the venture would end up being a disaster. Mycoskie, however, had faith that the space could be a commercial success. "I don't have research to prove this," he said at the time, "but the people who come here every day, over time, can't fight the human, compulsive desire to buy something. The harder you're selling them sometimes, the less effective you are as a retailer."[13]

As it turns out, TOMS' Venice Beach location was profitable within six months of opening and began returning cash to the company within eighteen months. It was such a success, in fact, that Mycoskie and his team opened another. Today they have six.

What Mycoskie and his team discovered was that by elevating the purpose of the retail space beyond the banality of transactional conversion, they had created a vehicle that was creating converts for their brand. And for the converted, TOMS ceased to be simply a shoe seller. It became a trusted and comforting aspect of their life and a reflection of their values.

Wittingly or not, TOMS had built a retail space that offers a glimpse into a future in which the store becomes a potent form of media.

17

The Store Is Media

AS ALL FORMS of media continue their evolution to becoming "the store," the actual places we call stores today will begin a corresponding transition toward becoming a powerful form of media. In fact, physical shopping spaces will ultimately prove to be the most powerful, immediate and measurable form of media available to a retailer or brand.

I say this for a few reasons. First, because physical spaces will allow consumers to have retailer- or brand-related experiences that cannot be fully replicated online, making them extremely special. Second, because in a world of fleeting and fragmented attention, shopping spaces are an opportunity for shoppers to be fully (cognitively, emotionally and physically) engaged in a branded media experience that no other media format can consistently promise. Moreover, these physical media experiences carry a high level of measurability because the consumer's engagement isn't implied or estimated, as it is with most forms of advertising media. Instead, with physical media we know for certain that the consumer is present inside the experience itself—their body is physically there!

It's anybody's guess whether someone saw your TV ad. It's harder to dispute that someone physically visited your retail space, and thanks to a growing variety of offline analytics tools, we can now easily and accurately measure these physical engagements. Most importantly, it's a scientific fact that the cognitive recall of physical experiences is far greater than the recall of passive experiences, such as those resulting from seeing or hearing advertisements.

The bottom line is that physical experiences are more powerful, more memorable and more measurable than any other form of media. Period. But in order for retailers to bridge the gap to the future, they will have to make a bold intellectual leap forward with respect to their beliefs about what a store is, what it does and how what it does is measured. For most, this leap means leaving the relative safety of what we know *isn't* working any longer and stepping into the realm of what we don't yet fully understand. In other words, it's time to blow up the paradigm of what a retail store is and has been and imagine instead what the retail store of the future can and will become.

What you'll find is that once we stop treating shopping spaces as product distribution points and begin approaching them as experiential media channels, every aspect of how we plan, design, build, operate and measure their success and effectiveness will implicitly change. And these changes will touch every stakeholder. The supplier/retailer relationship will transform, the role of the retail employee will evolve, the skill sets of retail executives will change entirely and the expectations of shareholders will modify based on a new retail reality.

We have to accept it. Retail, as we know it, is over.

Less inventory, more inventiveness

As technology increasingly blurs the lines between the digital and the physical, retailers need to look for all opportunities to dramatically lower the percentage of floor space allocated to products, packaging and merchandise displays and proportionately redeploy that space to instead offer unique experiences leveraging technology wherever it creates value to do so. It's important to note that these won't be mere novelty displays or installations but uses of technology that add significant utility or sheer delight to the shopper experience.

In a pre-digital world, the big-box retail business model made sense. Where else could you go to see so many products in one place? In a post-digital world, however, the assortments offered in a big-box store will look sadly diminutive when compared with sophisticated virtual marketplaces. Moreover, the shopper's ability to comfortably browse many of those products is limited by the realities of the big-box environment—like dodging forklifts.

The challenge for stores is to broaden their selection of products while offering more and better customer experiences, but to do so without the need for more inventory.

"We think of this [the store] as our largest product." ANGELA AHRENDTS

Virtually perfect

This challenge of allowing customers to better experience its products led Lowe's Home Improvement to begin reimagining how it could help customers plan and purchase items for their kitchen and bath projects. Starting with select stores in the Seattle area, Lowe's is working with Microsoft to incorporate the company's HoloLens mixed reality (MR) glasses into its kitchen departments.

With the aid of a well-trained in-store associate, customers can define the dimensions of their space, make some preliminary selections and then slip on a MR headset and literally walk into their virtual kitchen or bath project. From an iPad, the sales associate can view what a customer is seeing and make suggestions with regard to fixtures, finishes and layout, changing elements of the room on the fly. As changes are made, the customer gets a real-time view of the room as it transforms.

Shoppers will be able to truly visualize their own customized project to scale and make informed choices about the various elements, including taps, counters, sinks and cabinets. Not only does this approach make for a better experience than sorting through innumerable paint swatches, countertop materials and fixtures, it also makes infinitely better use of space in a Lowe's store.

Imagine how many experiences of this sort could ultimately play out in the big-box retail space of the future. Imagine if you could do a mixed reality walk through your plumbing repair, electrical job or landscaping project with a trained professional to show you how. Imagine if you could do a virtual walk through your own home, trying out and selecting new paint colors, flooring, fixtures and window coverings as you go. And all without ever leaving the store!

With the power of mixed reality, retail spaces themselves will become portals to a new experiential universe offering education, entertainment and immersive product trials.

Fewer "friends," but a lot more social

In the beginning, social media was sold to brands as a means of creating a community with their customers. This marketing strategy sounded fine, with one small hitch; it's not what consumers want. In fact, one study suggested that 55 percent of U.S. consumers and 63 percent of U.K. consumers have no interest whatsoever in following brands on social networks.[1] None.

As a consequence, many of these attempts to develop relationships with consumers and drive incremental business to retail have fallen flat. The result has led many marketers and even more chief financial officers to question the return on investment in social media.

What is undeniable, however, is that as consumers, we trust the opinions of others when it comes to products and services. In fact, while only 36 percent of us trust an ad we see on a social network, 92 percent of us trust a recommendation we see there from someone we know. Even more remarkable, 70 percent of us trust the opinions of complete and utter strangers!

In other words, the true power of social media doesn't lie in a brand's ability to speak to consumers; it lies in consumers' ability to speak to one another and learn what others think of a product or service.

What is also true is that this need to see social validation—what others think of a product—while shopping has become so embedded a touchstone that its absence can be disconcerting. How many of us would now be comfortable booking a hotel without knowing how it rates on TripAdvisor? Who would buy a car without reading an unbiased review—in *Consumer Reports,* for example? How many of us today would choose a movie without checking Rotten Tomatoes? Social proof and validation have simply become intrinsic aspects of our shopping behavior, linchpins in the decision process.

And yet when we walk into most retail environments, we are entering digital deserts that are barren of any meaningful social content at all. There's not even a hint of the reviews, ratings or other user-generated content that we have become so accustomed to incorporating into our buying behavior. In most cases, the only information we get to base a purchase on is a price sticker, a label and a full-time employee with a part-time interest in helping us. This is a huge gap.

In essence, our consumer brains have rapidly become post-digital but retail hasn't kept up. We are no longer shocked or surprised by the presence of technology or information. Instead, we're more surprised by its absence. This fact is creating an unprecedented level of cognitive dissonance for shoppers whose brains have become programmed to these online buying inputs. It's a gap that will only grow larger and more profound with time and even greater levels of connectedness.

Understanding that social proof is now an embedded navigation principle, the retailer of the future will treat this technology as an upfront design imperative. Using technology, retailers will give customers access to real-time ratings and reviews on every product they display in-store or online.

Some adventurous brands such as Nordstrom have already incorporated social proof into their stores by attaching "popular on Pinterest" tags to the products that are most popular on the social network. Apparel retailer C&A undertook a unique experiment in which Facebook likes for products were transmitted down to the actual hangers in stores so shoppers could see in real time how popular various items were. Other companies, such as Sephora, have been even bolder by enabling access to customer-generated product reviews for all products through their mobile app. And not surprisingly, Amazon, in its very first standalone brick-and-mortar bookstore in Seattle, was sure to bring product reviews directly to the shelf edge. Appearing just as they would on Amazon's website, signs display actual user reviews of each in-stock book.

Less permanent, more ephemeral

In the future, the concept of a store being a permanent, monolithic structure or destination will become outmoded. Technology will give brands and retailers the ability to take their offerings directly to the consumer, geographically and temporally. Whether through physical pop-up stores connected by digital systems or entirely virtual stores invisible to the naked eye, brands and retailers will transport spaces and experiences opportunistically to capitalize on audiences, events and occasions.

Malls, too, will shift their form and function, adding and deleting retailers, experiences and spaces within the space. Food courts will become the domain of food trucks, and other rotating concepts will add variety and interest to malls. A percentage of space in every mall will soon house an ever-changing lineup of retail and entertainment startups. New events, happenings and offerings will give shoppers reason to return regularly.

In a connected world, the retail space can be transported to wherever makes the most sense and can offer those products and experiences that are most contextually relevant for various audiences.

Swedish for uncommon sense

How do you bring your products and immersive brand experiences to consumers without making the customary investments in stores and inventory? If you're IKEA Canada, you take a small space on a busy street corner in Toronto and you invite consumers to shop virtually. Its 2015 pop-up store included virtual reality headsets that allowed shoppers to view and interact within entire IKEA kitchen sets. It also featured fifty different IKEA home products but had no carts, no shopping baskets and, above all, no inventory. Instead, customers were given a wooden spoon containing a radio-frequency identification (RFID) chip and invited to browse the store, tapping the spoon on the display items they wished to purchase. Once they were done, they simply took the spoon to the checkout, confirmed their order and paid. Their order was then picked and shipped the same day.

Beyond the obvious sales opportunities that pop-ups like this provide, there's also a powerful physical media value to taking the shop to the shopper. Not only can brands expose themselves to consumers outside their typical target segments, they can offer shoppers an immersive introduction to their brand story, products and shopping ecosystem.

Today, these sorts of installations are the exception. Soon, temporary and virtual shopping spaces will become the norm. In fact, even today, entire business verticals are developing to accommodate the anticipated growth of ephemeral retail.

For example, companies such as Storefront, whose clients include the likes of online disruptors Indochino and Ministry of Supply, specialize in assisting brands and retailers with finding temporary spaces. Rentals can range from a few months to a few hours depending on the client's needs.

And ShopWithMe is going even further by changing the concept of what a "store" is. The U.S.-based company manufactures what it calls micro automated retail stores (MARS). These fully digitalized, modular stores are customized for the needs of an individual retailer, programmed with its product catalog information and then leased out for whatever length of time they're required. Surfaces in the environment provide digital product information that can be edited on the fly, if necessary. And if the retailer changes its product assortment, there is no need to change the merchandising. The retailer just updates the software, and the store will change its form to accommodate.

Less physical, less digital, more phygital

The shopping experience of the future will cease to distinguish between the physical and the digital and will focus instead on the precise blend of both that is ideally suited to the moments along the customer's journey. Recognizing that all

A Sephora TIP (Teach, Inspire, Play) store.
IMAGE COURTESY OF SEPHORA

of the channels a customer passes through on that journey, be they virtual stores, mobile, physical stores, kiosks etc., have their own unique attributes, the best retailers will leverage each, alone or in combination, to create remarkable phygital experiences.

Technology will not be obtrusive or conspicuous within the shopping journey but will simply happen to be there when required to add value or remove friction.

The face of things to come

Few retailers have moved as boldly to incorporate technology into the customer experience as Sephora. Whereas many retailers were panicking because their customers were pulling out their smartphones in the aisle to gather information, read reviews and even buy products, the team at Sephora was beefing up their infrastructure to allow customers to do just that. According to Bridget Dolan, Sephora's U.S. vice president of innovation, it was never a question of the store *or* mobile but always a recognition that the two complement one another. "How can I expect our customer to use their mobile device constantly through the day but suddenly not use it when they come to our store?" she says.

The company's wildly successful mobile app has a high degree of functionality, which allows users to shop, experiment and play. For example, augmented reality makeup try-ons, random makeover recommendations and video tutorials on various makeup techniques all help shoppers discover new looks. The app also features a nifty thing called store mode, which lets shoppers indicate that they're in a store. The app instantly transforms to include a product scanner so they can read reviews or order online and access other functionality more related to being in a physical store.

For Dolan, decisions about where and when to inject technology into the experience are driven from deep analysis of the customer's journey and where along that journey technology can educate, inspire or allow for play. It's about "using each channel to the best of its ability and then combining them." Dolan adds that once the journey is understood, they will look for moments within the journey when technology can enhance the experience or alleviate friction.

She points to the fact that with more than two hundred brands and thousands of SKUs of product in-store, technology can be invaluable in helping to narrow the range of product options. "A lipstick has a scent to it, or a texture or a creaminess that is very hard to discern with virtual technology. However, I could stand in a store with a phone in my hand and virtually try on 3,000 lipsticks until I find the 5 that I want to try on physically in-store."[2]

Sephora's new TIP (Teach, Inspire, Play) stores are a perfect example of the new phygital experience—the elegant blend of physical and digital. "We've designed the experience to be enhanced by technology if you want technology or to avoid technology if that's how you want to shop,"[3] Dolan says. Shoppers can come to the store to work with an in-store expert, take an online class or just play and experiment on their own using iPad-based tutorials. They can take inspiration from the content that Sephora provides and also explore various looks and techniques posted by other Sephora customers. Unlike so many stores where the cash wrap is the focal point of the design, Sephora has put its Teach, Inspire, Play area front and center, inviting customers to stay, try its products and have fun.

For Sephora and other future-minded retailers, technology doesn't get bolted onto the customer experience; it is seamlessly woven into it. Decisions about which technologies will be used and how they will be used will always originate from the needs of the customer. Dolan confides that there are times when a particularly cool technology will catch her eye. Nonetheless, she'll always dig deeper to ask how "the application of that technology" might make her customer's journey easier or more delightful. If it will do neither, it doesn't make the cut.

Less omnichannel, more moments

We will soon, thankfully, stop talking about "omnichannel" customer experiences. This will be good news for the millions of us whose minds have been numbed by the sight of the word on a decade's worth of PowerPoint slides. Omnichannel will soon be taken out to the retail jargon scrap heap. In truth, there really is no longer such a thing as an omnichannel customer experience, largely because shoppers no longer consciously experience brands in channels. Instead, a customer's experience comprises moments: moments of discovery, moments of interest, moments of need and moments of trial, to name a few. And it's in these moments that a retailer will exceed expectations, meet expectations or fail miserably.

Moreover, because we are rapidly moving toward a future in which every piece of media in the market becomes a direct portal to purchase and in which everything around us becomes connected and intelligent, it's safe to assume that digital will no longer be merely *a* channel for consumption; rather, it will be *the* channel. We will no longer use the term "digital commerce." Just commerce.

Where retail today is 10 to 15 percent online and 85 to 90 percent in-store, within two decades these numbers will be reversed. Most goods will be sold through some connected means and most shopping will happen through some mobile form. Even today, an estimated 64 percent of all in-store transactions are being impacted by digital in some way,[4] so it's reasonable to assume that within a decade or two the vast majority of all commerce will be digital.

Unlike today, physical retail spaces will no longer be the end point in the consumer's journey but the beginning. The physical experience will be the catalyst for the consumer's long-term digital relationship with the brand. The store will be the powerful physical, emotional and intellectual nitroglycerine that sets off a deep affiliation with a brand across the moments of a consumer's life. Most of these moments, however, will be digitally connected.

So, rather than approaching the new customer experience from a channel perspective (mobile app, web, store, social, etc.), retailers must instead begin to consider every single moment of engagement between their brands and a consumer as a moment of truth. It may be a moment in which the consumer discovers a retailer's brand on a social network, sees its logo on a billboard, meets a friend who's wearing one of its items or views one of its products placed in a movie.

The first step is to truly understand each of these specific moments and the consumer need that lies deep within it. The next step is to ensure that each and every one of these moments of brand/consumer contact is treated as an opportunity to not only deliver the right information, tools and facility to meet the need, but also to enable the consumer to buy what you sell with confidence in that exact moment. How that's executed has less to do with any specific *channels* and more to do with the customer's likely location, context and temporal state. Where are they? What are they doing? And how much time do they have? What you deliver to them, how and in what format(s) will depend on their specific intent and state in the moment. Lastly, retailers will need to connect these moments by linking all customer data to a central point where it can be easily accessed as necessary to allow customers to move fluidly through their journey with the brand.

This lofty goal of executing brilliantly in every potential moment of a consumer's life with your business is ambitious to say the least, and not as easy as buying an off-the-shelf solution from a technology provider. It's a process that begins by developing a deep understanding of the customer's journey with your brand. Once the journey is meticulously mapped, deciding on the combination of technologies, resources and delivery methods that will best serve them in that moment will be infinitely easier.

Living in the moment

At Recreational Equipment, Inc. (REI), every decision, including which products to sell, is distilled from painstaking insights arising from the customer experience. According to Brad Brown, REI's senior vice president of digital retail, it's a process that starts with one hell of a long sheet of paper. On that sheet of paper, Brown and his team detail everything they know, think they know and wonder about the customer journey from "customer research, with moments of truth of the buying journey, with pain points and with opportunities."[5] To make the point,

Brown displays one such map just for the footwear journey that stretches the entire length of a conference room wall.

Maps like this become the basis for development of all digital solutions, store operations, marketing decisions and retail designs. Everything is focused on the customer's moment-to-moment journey with the brand and their specific needs within each moment. It's precisely this heavy lifting that many companies aspiring to "omnichannel" retailing fail to do, and the reason that so many such efforts spin their wheels. At REI, more than a quarter of sales now happen digitally, but the company recognizes that the other 75 percent of sales that occur in their stores are heavily influenced by digital. Therefore, the going-in assumption is that the company's digital assets have to be flexible and functional across each potential moment in the journey.

One small but important example of this effort to deliver on moments has been REI's work to turn every media experience into a buying opportunity by "deep linking" the content in its mobile app. Deep linking means giving REI app users the ability to open pages on the app directly from any other media they may come across. If REI customers encounter an REI product on any digital media, they can click it and be brought to that specific product page within the app. On that page is all the information and functionality they require to buy the item immediately, if they choose. Or shoppers might instead choose to locate the nearest store, check inventory and simply go to the store to pick up the products they want. While at the store, they can use the app to scan and read reviews of other products, which they may opt to buy online rather than carrying home that day. REI staff, or Green Vests, as they're called, also carry mobile clienteling technology that allows them to access product and inventory data as well as details about individual customer loyalty rewards.

For Elizabeth Dowd, REI's divisional vice president of retail experience, and her colleagues, the key to developing these customer experiences is breaking down each of those moments on the journey map into their smallest components and then understanding the combination of technology, information and in-store production required to exceed customer expectations. That process, according to Dowd, is highly cross-functional, with technology staff working shoulder to shoulder with marketing and store operations staff. Each store experience, for example, is fully staged at the REI Workshop—an industrial space in Seattle where sales staff, customers and other REI team members can walk through the experience and provide feedback.

Even buying activity, usually a top-down exercise, is driven by the design of the customer experience. Dowd tells me that she's even been known to buy outside products with her own credit card and add them to an experiential design if she thinks those products will help make for a better customer experience. In fact, it's not unusual, according to Dowd, for many of these supplemental products to eventually make their way into the brand's core assortment. For REI and other future-focused retailers, great customer experience does not happen in channels; it happens in moments. Moments to discover, try, inspire and buy.

The Future
of Retail

SO CONTRARY TO what some are saying, the future of retail is
bright. Online experiences will become more physical and tan-
gible in nature, and amazing physical shopping spaces will
be supported by great technology that adds fluidity and value.
Both kinds of shopping experiences will be commercially viable
and coexist well into the future. The same rosy outlook, however, cannot be afforded to the traditional economic relationship between retailers and their vendors—otherwise known
as wholesale sales. It is my belief that wholesale, as a model, is
nearing its breaking point.

Consider the way this age-old relationship looks from both
sides. For retailers, it means buying product in significant volume, distributing it to their stores, merchandising it, pricing
it, uploading data about it, training staff on it and advertising
it. If they're lucky they sell it, but they will still inevitably take
some of it back in the form of returns. And they do all of this
while clinging to the hope that they can eke out a profit between
wholesale cost and retail price. It's a gamble at the best of times.

But here's the thing: today a growing percentage of the brands these retailers carry are not only selling to directly competing online marketplaces, they are also aggressively opening their own vertically integrated stores. The retailers' own vendors are becoming their fiercest competitors. It's hardly an ideal relationship.

But before we go branding vendors as the villains, the wholesale relationship doesn't look much sunnier from their standpoint either. Vendors are asked to supply on time and in full against wildly fluctuating customer demand or suffer penalties. They are asked by retailers for increased allowances and advertising dollars, and often made to swallow their own price increases or face being replaced. And what do they get for these pains? Retailers have been known to bait customers with brands, only to switch them over to private label products. Even worse, some brands have been all but drained of any equity through excessive retail discounting and shoddy customer experiences. It's not exactly optimal either.

The whole exercise points to a relationship that's untenable going forward. Retailers will no longer be able to compete against marketplaces or their own brand partners' direct selling. At the same time, brands will no longer be willing to depend on retailers to adequately uphold their brand perception, customer experience expectations, price integrity and goals for market penetration. The result will be a bifurcation in the market that will lead to a completely new economic model between brands and retailers. Retail, especially in the highly vulnerable mid-tier price range, will essentially split into two very distinct factions.

If it can go direct, it will

Today, it's estimated that at least 40 percent of consumer brands sell direct to consumers in some manner,[1] a number that's growing rapidly. Nike, for example, has made it abundantly clear that it intends to grow its direct-to-consumer business by at least 250 percent, or from $6.6 billion to $16 billion over the next five years. In 2016, more than 23 percent of total sales at Nike were generated through direct-to-consumer channels.[2] Likewise, fashion brand Kate Spade New York reported a 28 percent increase in direct-to-consumer sales in the fourth quarter of 2014. Other brands, such as luxury goods maker Coach, for example, are threatening to pull out of department stores entirely, in favor of better controlling their destiny through their own branded stores.

Beyond the established brands, a steady stream of startups is completely foregoing any relationship with retail distribution in favor of a direct relationship with customers. The ability to tailor assortments for small market segments and reach those segments directly through multiple channels is making retail distribution unnecessary for many.

For example, Stowaway Cosmetics is a startup company that offers a line of "right-sized" products for women that fit easily in the average handbag and can be used completely before their expiration date. After learning that three-quarters of women never finish using their makeup products before they expire, co-founders Chelsa Crowley and Julie Fredrickson set out to disrupt the quantity and size paradigm. By avoiding retail entirely, the pair was able to sell their half-sized products at half the price. Brands such as Stowaway can strip additional costs out of their businesses by eschewing traditional advertising, relying instead on social buzz and influencer marketing.

All this change has already led to some very uncomfortable conversations between brands and their retail partners, many of which regard the direct-to-market approach as a betrayal and an attack. But it's important to keep a couple of things in mind. First, direct sales don't represent a departure from business norms. They are a return to the way things were for centuries.

Manufacturers and their customers have always enjoyed a very natural and fitting relationship. After all, who could possibly know the product more intimately than the very people who make it, and who could guard the brand's reputation more earnestly than the makers themselves? Second, a study recently found that more than 50 percent of customers who visit a brand or manufacturer's website do so with the intent to purchase directly.

Retail, as we know it today, was largely a by-product of the Industrial Revolution, which was a necessary construct for manufacturers hoping to reach expanding urban markets. Retail distribution allowed such manufacturers to spread the risk of reaching those mass markets. The more layers of distribution, the lower the individual level of risk for each member of the supply chain. As markets grew, so too did the layers of distribution. In the twentieth century, those layers acted as lubricant in reaching and satisfying markets. Yet now they have become increasingly unnecessary layers of friction.

Today, it is not only possible for brands to serve individual customers directly, it's often preferred. After all, each time a product moves down through another rung of distribution, markups (often as much as 100 percent) are added. By the time a twenty-dollar pair of shoes makes it to the consumer, it might cost one hundred dollars or more. And now manufacturers are beginning to ask, "For what?"

And if retailers think their relationships with brands are tough now, just wait until the full impact of all the technologies I've mentioned truly comes to bear. Imagine how different the market will look when a sensor reorders a new pair of shoes directly from Nike when they wear out. Or when I can order more Oreos by saying the word "Oreos" to my personal digital assistant. Or when artificial intelligence and predictive algorithms manage most of my day-to-day needs.

There was a time when, if your aim as a brand was to reach customers en masse, wholesale distribution was a necessary evil. To reach many people, you needed many sources of distribution. In a new age, however, where a one-to-many model for sales is not only feasible for brands but increasingly preferred, the age of wholesale will steadily come to a close.

Rise of the experiential retailer

So, expect to see a steady cleaving off in the market as an increasing number of brands take their fate and their customers directly into their own hands and their own stores. They will craft exclusive experiences that will focus on deep levels of brand storytelling and intense product engagement.

That said, consumers will also crave the ability to experience multiple brands within a given category. But as I've pointed out, we will also expect unique and engaging experiences at the same time. This will give rise to an entirely new breed of *experiential retailer* that goes extremely deep within a category of goods and creates extraordinary experiences for consumers across a range of brands or products.

Part media outlet, part sales agent, part design firm, experiential retailers will use their physical shopping spaces to perfect the consumer experience across a category or categories of products. They will define and design the ideal experiential journey and they will employ expert "product ambassadors" and technology to deliver something truly unique, remarkable and memorable. So memorable, in fact, that it leaves a lasting experiential imprint on the shopper.

The sole aim of these new-era retailers will be to drive significant sales for the brands they represent across every available channel. But unlike stores of today, which are single-mindedly focused on keeping sales in-house, shopping spaces of the future will position themselves as true "everychannel" hubs. That is, they will serve customers through multiple means of fulfill-ment that will ultimately include themselves, their vendors and their competitors—yes, even their competitors. Who makes these sales, how and when, will matter less than delivering the powerful shopping experience responsible for generating them. Freed from the shackles of per-square-foot sales, experiential retailers will treat shoppers to a wide array of products, includ-ing prototypes from major brands and startups.

Skids of products and rows of shelving will give way to bril-liantly creative spatial designs and artful merchandising, allow-ing space for media and total interaction with products. Social media will be infused into the experience, offering at-the-shelf reviews, ratings and product comparisons. The space will become an immersive and experiential advertisement for the products it represents and a direct portal to the entire universe of distribution channels available.

Retailers that can design and execute these outstanding cus-tomer experiences will not be satisfied to eke out a meager mar-gin; instead, they will charge brands an upfront fee, or "card rate," based on the volume of positive exposure they bring to the brands and products they represent in-store. And brands will willingly pay to have their products represented and their unique stories told in these remarkable physical retail media spaces of the future.

This is story

On Manhattan's Lower West Side sits what I consider to be a two-thousand-square-foot glimpse into the future of retail. STORY is the brainchild of Rachel Shechtman, a charismatic entrepreneur with a background in both retail and market-ing. STORY is a space that, as Shechtman puts it, has "the point of view of a magazine, everything changes every four to eight weeks like a gallery, and it sells things like a store."[3]

Founder Rachel Shechtman says that STORY on New
York City's West side "takes the point of view of a magazine,
changes like a gallery and sells things like a store."
COURTNEY OF STORY

Shechtman also subscribes religiously to the notion that
retail can and should be a powerful form of media. She told the
New York Times, "When you look at the square footage certain
brands occupy, and you look at the amount of time consumers
spend in those spaces, why isn't that a media channel?" The time
spent shopping in a store, she continued, "is more than the 30
seconds spent flipping through the pages of a magazine."[4]

Shechtman points to the fact that while technology is completely reinventing the way we shop online, the retail industry
as a whole has been woefully lacking when it comes to reinventing how we shop offline. Retailers have done very little to
quantify, much less monetize the experiences they create for
customers in their spaces. But monetizing experiences is precisely what Shechtman and her team at STORY do. And they do
it between eight and twelve times each year. Put simply, brands
pay STORY to tell their stories.

Shechtman has created a variety of stories for brands such as
Gillette, GE, Home Depot and American Express. It's not unusual

for brands, which Shechtman calls editors, to spend a minimum of $400,000 to work with her to create a story. It may be a story about love, travel, men, women or any number of other themes that showcase and truly celebrate the products on display—most of which are sold on a consignment basis.

And while big brands are one part of the equation, STORY also feeds the city's grassroots business community by holding pitch nights during which local artisans, small manufacturers and craftspeople can make a case for why STORY should feature their products.

Shechtman acknowledges that STORY's concept might not be suited to every market, but she nonetheless feels that brands are ignoring a tremendous opportunity to use stores as a media channel. "Starbucks gets 55 million people into its stores in the U.S. every week. Target gets 30 million a month. Those are major impressions. When you look at that at scale with so many other retailers, why aren't brands doing more in those spaces and looking at it as a marketing and advertising tool and not just about consumption?"[5]

But how do you measure the impact and value of a *story*? As it turns out, Shechtman has equipped the space with technology that measures the customer's journey through the store and the specific elements of each curated presentation that they're interacting with. For customers, she says, the store is about having fun; for brands, it's about providing backend data and analytics on how their products and content are being received. In short, STORY is a powerful, and measurable form of physical, interactive brand media.

Despite Shechtman's success with STORY, many in retail's old guard have been quick to pooh-pooh the concept as a novelty that can't apply in the "real world" of retail. With that in mind, I was interested to hold Shechtman's media model up to the harsh light of conventional retail metrics. What if, I wondered, we were to compare the sales performance per square foot of STORY to an average Macy's location?

Here are my loose and, I confess, largely unscientific numbers.

STORE	STORE SIZE	GROSS ANNUAL REVENUE (EST.)	REVENUE/SQ. FT.
STORY	2,000 sq. ft.	$4,200,000*	$2,100
Macy's (avg.)	150,000 sq. ft.**	$27,000,000	$180[6]

* Estimate based on eight reported branded stories annually at an average of $525K in revenue each, net of any consignment sales.
** Size based on new smaller-footprint stores.

So, with its "retail as media" model, STORY's per-square-foot sales exceed Macy's by nearly twelve times.

Then, I wondered, what would happen if even *half* of an average Macy's store adopted a similar "store as media" model? What could the effect be on its total revenue? And just to be realistic, I discounted the extraordinary per-square-foot revenue rate of STORY by approximately 50 percent, allowing for the greater floor space of a Macy's and other potential variables. Here is my projection of Macy's revenue with 50 percent of its floor space dedicated to "retail as media."

MODEL	GROSS REVENUE	COMBINED TOTAL
½ store current conventional sales model @$180 sales revenue/sq. ft.	$13,500,000	$96,000,000
½ store with "retail as media" model @$1,100 sales revenue/sq. ft.	$82,500,000	

In this scenario, this single Macy's location would go from generating $27 million in sales to $96 million in combined sales and retail media revenue, an incremental difference of $69 million annually—in just one store.

And for the realists out there; even if one were to experientialize just one-quarter of the Macy's store, the incremental lift would still be almost $35 million! More importantly, the company would achieve this increase, not by adding more inventory, not by hiring legions of new people and not by buying more advertising. Macy's would do it by working with vendors in a new way to create something together that customers absolutely love!

Would this retail media model work for *all* Macy's stores? Likely not. But with a potential revenue lift of roughly 350 percent in one store alone, it wouldn't have to work in many locations to completely rejuvenate the chain's business.

What Macy's has in its stores is a consumer audience. What it needs now is remarkable experiential theater to delight them!

Retail as data

This new experiential model will require retailers not only to qualify but also to quantify the experience they deliver, the traffic they generate and the consequent downstream sales impact they influence. It won't be enough to talk in fluffy terms about customer delight and engagement. Experiential retailers will need to know who comes to their stores, whether they are unique or repeat visitors, where they go, what they engage with and for how long, and what actions result from their visit. They will need to measure not only the presence of the shoppers but also the aggregate response of shoppers to the experience.

To that end, an array of technologies will enable a 360-degree understanding of the moment-by-moment experience in both stores and the centers in which they sit. Unlike today, however, many more of these technologies will be used to pull valuable behavioral information and attitudinal data from shoppers as opposed to pushing offers, discounts and promotions. Unlike the blunt instruments of today, experiential retailers will use these technologies with surgical precision in the retail spaces of the future.

Technologies such as:

→ **anonymous facial recognition** to develop an aggregate view of the traffic level in a space and the demographic profile of the audience, allowing retail teams to adapt the environmental conditions (lighting, music, displays, experiences) in real time.

→ **beacon technology** to understand what information consumers are most in need of or pulling from specific categories, products and displays within the store.

→ **emotional tracking** to pinpoint aspects of the store experience that leave shoppers happy, bored, frustrated or confused, allowing experiential designers to edit the space in real time.

→ **fitting room technologies** to determine which brands or products, sizes and styles are being tried on and when fed through big data analytics, to power coordinating product recommendations and inform predictive category buying analytics.

→ **interactive signage and tagging** to customize messaging and even pricing depending on shopper demographics and loyalty status.

→ **membership or subscriber identification** to connect the experience in the store to a later purchase made via mobile or another channel.

→ **mobile engagement** to reveal what information consumers are gathering by scanning products in-store and the impact that supporting information has on immediate or latent purchase.

→ **mobile identification tracking** to identify unique versus repeat visitors to the store and average dwell times, using the Bluetooth signal from smart devices.

→ **radio-frequency identification (RFID)** to establish a picture of which products are being viewed, handled or abandoned most often.
→ **sales associate engagement and clienteling** to capture the most common shopper queries and changes in individual shopper tastes and preferences, allowing analysts to anticipate future trends.
→ **video analytics** to understand guest navigation patterns through the space, allowing designers to modify elements of the store to enhance the experience.

Clearly, the level of data produced by physical retail spaces is astonishing and carries tremendous value, not only for retailers but also for the brands they partner with.

With this knowledge in mind, another class of experiential retailer will earn revenue solely by monetizing these enormous streams of consumer data that their stores capture each day. This will include data about who came to the store and whether they were new or repeat visitors. Information about what they looked at, what they interacted with and for how long—and ultimately what the consequences of these interactions ended up being. Did the customers eventually buy something? If so, what did they buy, and when and where did they buy it? Did they share their experience with others? If so, through which social channels? These experiential retailers will use their spaces as living websites to capture and catalog all these aspects of the experience and more. And they will charge brands for access to and interpretation of this data and of the conversation that circulates around their product in-store and even downstream of the store experience.

Currently in b8ta

Almost three thousand miles away from STORY and the mean streets of New York, a small store in Palo Alto, California called

Using advanced offline analytic technologies, b8ta stores monitor and measure all consumer interaction with in-store products.
B8TA

b8ta is also charting a course for the future of retail. B8ta, which opened in 2016, specializes in showcasing a unique range of connected devices from manufacturers ranging from Fortune 500 brands to little-known startups. The result is a truly unique mix of products that you're never likely to see in your local Best Buy. But apart from its products, what makes b8ta truly unusual is its business model. The company makes almost 100 percent of its revenue by monetizing the consumer data that is generated and captured within its walls.

The concept began when four former Nest employees, Vibhu Norby, Phillip Raub, William Mintun and Nick Mann, concluded that retail was fundamentally a broken model. Products, they felt, took too long to get into stores, and many of the most interesting products would never get picked up because they weren't proven sellers. Moreover, most retail stores didn't afford shoppers the ability to play with products or learn and experience what they could do, largely because most were filled with nonworking product displays and boxes of inventory. These glaring flaws in the retail model inspired them to open b8ta.

The mission at b8ta is not to sell, but rather to treat customers to the best possible product experience. The small space is designed as a geek's paradise—a mini-gallery of awesome and innovative technology products. From robots and drones to connected home devices, you'll find things at b8ta you didn't know existed. Each product has its own dedicated space, digital merchandiser and connected signage that displays information about the product as well as its price. In addition, experienced, friendly staff are on hand to work with customers one on one.

Moreover, b8ta connects brands directly to their products in-store, allowing them to control the marketing information, pricing and training materials associated with their product. This ability for brands to tweak the information and pricing of their products—particularly new products—in real time adds an entirely new layer of research and market testing capability.

But the most significant difference between b8ta and traditional retailers is that their retail space is, in essence, a living website where everything that happens within it is captured and recorded to become part of an analytics package that is delivered in real time to its brands and manufacturing partners on a subscription basis. Brands learn who, in an aggregate sense, engaged with their products, how they engaged with them and for how long—the exact real-time insights that brands, and particularly startup ventures, would find invaluable. Phillip Raub, b8ta co-founder, tells me that his team is also currently working on methods to connect the in-store experience with downstream purchases to truly close the loop.

Raub points out that the dwell-time metrics in the store are particularly long compared to other electronics stores, which I noticed myself when I visited the store shortly after its opening.

Shoppers seemed to move from one product to the next, trying almost everything, like kids in a toy store.

CEO and co-founder Vibhu Norby believes that retail "will ultimately be a marketing function and not a sales function. That's what vendors are paying for at b8ta, [thousands of] people a month trying and seeing their products for the first time."[7]

In other words, the store of the future will not only monetize experiences but also the data that those experiences generate.

Fewer clerks, more brand ambassadors

And with retail's future pointing in an entirely new direction, what does that future hold for retail employees? Well, there's just no way to put it gently. The days of the retail clerk are over. By clerk, I'm referring to the millions of retail workers who operate checkouts, greet customers at the door, count inventory, look up prices, scan bar codes, corral shopping carts and do their best to remember snippets of product information about the vast assortments they carry. These jobs will all but disappear within twenty years, perhaps sooner.

Part of what's driving this change is the quickly growing gap between customer service expectations and reality. A recent survey indicated that a full 48 percent of shoppers today believe that they know more about the product they're looking for than the sales associate helping them,[8] and chances are they're right. It's never been easier to rapidly gather knowledge about specific products.

More startling, though, is that 67 percent of those surveyed have doubts about whether the sales associate helping them is even telling the truth. I suspect this has less to do with consumer paranoia and more to do with living in a world where the correct answer to any question is two clicks away. We trust Google infinitely more than we trust salespeople. And so, in a world where being partly right is as good as being wrong, the relative utility of retail salespeople is diminished. In fact, according to research released by Google, two-thirds of shoppers said they've been unable to find the information they need in stores,[9] resulting in almost half of them being left feeling frustrated.

Exacerbating the situation is the ongoing battle for higher wages by retail and hospitality workers. Few would defend the miserably low wages that retail has become notorious for paying. In the U.S., for example, the median wage for all retail workers in 2015 was $10.47 per hour,[10] or $21,780 per year. In the same year, the poverty threshold for a U.S. family of four was set at $24,250.[11] In other words, for at least 50 percent of retail workers, supporting a family with a spouse and two children on a retail salary implicitly means living in poverty.

You might expect such a low income to insulate retail workers from technological disruption, but it actually makes them much more vulnerable. Here's why. While the federal minimum wage is currently stuck at $7.25 per hour (some states have minimums that sit slightly above that), labor groups have been fighting for a mandated fifteen dollars per hour. Two U.S. states, New York and California, have already signed bills to move the minimum wage to fifteen dollars and an additional nine U.S. cities have approved moves to a fifteen-dollar minimum, some by as early as 2017.

The problem inherent in this increase is twofold. First, most economists agree that even a fifteen-dollar-per-hour minimum wage falls short of what it really should be if wages are properly indexed to inflation. Therefore, it's likely that the push to fifteen dollars is only a stepping-stone in what will be ongoing pressure to raise minimums even further. And while raising wages is the morally correct thing to do, it doesn't follow that there could possibly be a reciprocal increase in individual productivity to meet it. In other words, the nature and productivity of the work

SoftBank Robotics' Pepper robot is equipped to respond to
shoppers' basic questions and detect their emotional state.
SOFTBANK ROBOTICS

at nine dollars per hour is likely to be no different than at fifteen
dollars. The difference will have to be accounted for in either
lower corporate profits or higher consumer prices. Sure, we
can argue the bigger ethical questions that surround corporate
and consumer greed, but none of it solves the problem at hand.

Second, compounding the case against workers is the fact
that an army of technologies stands at the ready to take over
their work. For example, California-based Simbe Robotics
recently introduced its Tally robot, the world's first fully autonomous stock-keeping robot. Able to operate for between eight
and twelve hours on a single charge, Tally robots patrol the aisles
of grocery stores visually checking and recording up to twenty
thousand products at a shot, and they do so with near-perfect
accuracy. They then relay this information to store management
for action or correction. The robots can detect even the sub-
tlest shelving errors or out of stocks. According to Mirza Shah,

Simbe's chief technology officer, companies such as CVS or Walgreens would have to dedicate between twenty-five and forty staffing hours per week to accomplish the same amount of work as Tally, but even then, humans would complete it with far less accuracy.

New England–based robotics company Symbotic LLC makes robotic autonomous warehousing technology that can race through warehouse aisles and literally climb racking to put orders together in a fraction of the time it takes human workers. As a result, the technology can cut labor costs by up to 80 percent and reduce the warehouse footprint by 25 to 40 percent. Target is now using this technology in one of its largest distribution centers in California.

If you're thinking that inventory and warehouse jobs are more suited to robotics but that the sales associate role requires the human touch, Lowe's suggests otherwise. Following two years of testing robots in its Orchard Supply Hardware store in San Jose, California, the company recently announced that it would be introducing of a "fleet" of robots in its San Francisco area stores. The robots, called LoweBots, are programmed to greet customers at the door, respond in multiple languages, field product inquiries and direct customers to the items they're looking for. In addition, store staff can access the LoweBots for up-to-the-minute information on pricing or inventory. Moreover, the robots are able to analyze data and detect patterns that might influence business decisions in real time. And all without ever taking a lunch break, a sick day or even a paycheck!

But what if a customer isn't sure what product they want or need? Can technology help them find exactly the right product? That's precisely the problem Mumbai-based Fluid AI set out to solve when it partnered with IBM and U.S. retailer The

North Face to create an artificial intelligence–powered shopping bot called Expert Personal Shopper (xps). Using ibm Watson as the brains, Fluid created a customer service interface with which customers can find the perfect jacket simply by answering a series of questions posed by the application. Using natural speech processing, the app gradually narrows down the wide assortment of available products. For example, you can begin by saying, "I need a jacket for a trip to Vermont in the late fall." From there, the program will ask you a variety of relevant questions. It may ask you what activities you plan to do. Or it may inquire about the weight of jacket you'd prefer. As you answer each question, the ai will modify the potential recommendations, eventually landing on a few suggested products that meet each of the criteria you've indicated. And it will only get better, because the more people use the program, the smarter it becomes. ibm was so impressed that it acquired Fluid's xps technology in October of 2016.

And if you're among those who believe that our innate empathy and sensitivity to emotion is what safeguards humans from obsolescence at the hands of technology, it's important to know that SoftBank Robotics is building emotional sensitivity into its humanoid robot, Pepper. Pepper will not only respond to commands but will do so with sensitivity to the emotional state of its user.

While Steve Carlin, SoftBank Robotics' vice president, agrees that these are powerful new technologies, he in no way considers them precursors to any sort of robot apocalypse. At least for now, he sees the use of robots in the retail environment as limited to low-level operational tasks such as helping customers navigate the store or gathering basic information about products or services. He doesn't anticipate scores of robots displacing people in stores anytime soon.

Yet, according to a recent study from Oxford University, the impact of robots and AI on retail employment may be coming sooner than most of us think. In examining the likelihood of different types of workers being replaced by technology, the study determined that there is a 92 percent probability of frontline retail workers being technologized over the coming decade.[12] So, retailers everywhere will face difficult decisions in the years to come.

It stands to reason that companies like Walmart will be watching such technologies with great interest. After all, consider that the company employs more than 1.3 million associates in more than four thousand U.S. stores. The potential cost savings from technologizing even a small percentage of that sales force would be astronomical. And Walmart is not alone. The retail sector is North America's largest employer, accounting for more than 15 million workers, and in an industry continually challenged for profitability, the potential upside of replacing workers with technology has to be tantalizing.

Automate this!

But all this is not to say that we will soon be shopping in dystopian future stores devoid of people. In fact, while robotics and AI can be superior to humans at executing repetitive and linear tasks, there are as many things that they are poor at.

For one thing, robots tend to have weak fine-motor skills, making the manipulation and demonstration of complex objects or tasks very difficult and slow. Therefore, as retail spaces become more experiential in nature, they'll require human beings to operate and demonstrate products for consumers. And artificial intelligence, while tremendous at retrieving factual data and solving linear problems, is not so adept at intuiting creative and sometimes lateral solutions, much less forging an emotional connection with a customer. Technology, on its own, tends not to be the optimal solution.

Above all else, what humans bring to the table is their humanity. The retail workers of the future will be creative problem solvers who use lateral thinking to assist customers. They will be adept with technology and employ clienteling and other technologies to expertly guide shoppers and personalize recommendations. The retail associates of the future will be brand ambassadors—enthusiastic super-users of the products that the retailer trades in—who can speak with customers from first-hand experience. They will be the ultimate personification of the brand.

And for all this, the retail associates of the future will not need to protest or picket for a living wage. Instead, they will have employers falling over themselves to pay them well because the retail shopping space of the future will marry the efficiency and effectiveness of technology with the expertise, enthusiasm, empathy and creativity of outstanding human beings. Retail will cease to be the *job* it has become and reclaim its rightful place as a *profession* people can be proud to pursue.

19

A Bright New Era

IF A REVOLUTION of this magnitude in retail seems implausible, and you can't imagine a world where experiences become the primary source of retail revenue, I invite you to consider the economic transformation of the music industry. Twenty years ago, major recording artists made most of their revenue from record sales. In fact, musicians used to play live only to sell more records. Today, a mere 6 percent of the average recording artist's income is derived from record sales. Ninety-four percent comes from other activities, not the least of which are live performances and appearances. The model has been completely reversed.

So, too, will great retailers build more of their economic models with the idea of delivering and measuring live in-store experiences around their products rather than relying solely on the ever-diminishing margin from the sale of those products. Experiences will, in essence, become the product and the primary category that great retailers trade in.

In the long term, the relationship between brands and retailers, which has for so long been adversarial, will be reinvented. There will be no more contentious buyer/vendor negotiations over product pricing. No playing hardball for incentives or marketing dollars. No penalties for brands that don't meet expectations. In the approaching retail media era, the retailer will no longer be the customer of the brand. On the contrary, the brand will become the client of the retailer. You read that right. Retailers will work for their brands, and those who deliver results will command a fortune for doing so.

Above all, shoppers will enjoy a new and remarkable landscape where retail is once again made magical. Where theater and technology combine to form outstanding and memorable moments. A bright new era of retail in which every shopping space is a flagship.

PART

4

REENGINEERING RETAIL

Engineering
the Future

⋅⋅⋅⋅×⋅⋅⋅⋅

WHETHER YOU'RE AN online pure-play retailer or a chain with five thousand brick-and-mortar stores, you, like the rest of us, face a retail future that will bear virtually no resemblance to retail today. The concept of what a store is, how consumers buy and even the economic model for retail itself will change radically in the years and decades ahead. Retail is indeed being entirely reengineered.

Experiences will be the *product* of the future, and for many retailers the only hope of earning sustainable revenue. Retailers that can masterfully create memorable experiences will generate infinitely more revenue than was ever conceivable from relying solely on product sales. Some will use these experiences to catalyze product sales across their ecosystem of purchase points; others will monetize the experiences themselves.

Will your business be a vital part of this reengineered future of retail or merely a footnote in its history? The choice will ultimately be yours. I'm a huge believer in visioning—the idea that if you can envision a desired future state, you can realize that future state. If you're able to envision the future that this book points to, then I believe your likelihood of transitioning to that future is significant. The question is how best to initiate that transition.

In speaking with companies that are already actively reengineering retail, what I have realized is that there is no *one best way*. No single company purports to have the future completely figured out. There are no *rules of retail*, so to speak. That said, there are clear commonalities among those brands, retailers and technology companies that dare to push the envelope of what's possible.

The most important of these is that they accept the harsh yet oddly liberating reality that no one really needs what they sell. They recognize that in a pre-digital world, a consumer's biggest challenge was scarcity. The search for alternative products, brands and retailers could be difficult. Mediocre brands relied on this fact to survive. In a post-digital world, however, scarcity will cease to be an issue. Consumers will not only have infinite choice at their fingertips but also ever-present technology to help sift through it all instantly to find what's best for them.

Any business that relies on scarcity of alternatives as its competitive crutch will have a very rough ride ahead. You might obsess over your product and its nuanced superiority relative to your competitors, but the truth is that if you went out of business tomorrow, the wound would likely heal and consumers would find a substitute for your product quite easily. Unless you're fortunate enough to sell patented pharmaceuticals or some other remarkably unique product, you're facing the same reality we all face: no one needs *what* you sell. That's the bad news.

The good news is that the world desperately needs *how* you sell what you sell—the unique, remarkable and ownable experience you design around your product. How you sell what you sell is what will ultimately set you apart from competitors and win the hearts of consumers. How you sell what you sell will create the intangible value that consumers are willing to spend more of their money on. And how you sell what you sell will make your business indispensable to your customers.

While the need to create remarkable experiences may sound like something to be taken for granted, consider how few companies are truly differentiated in how they do business. Most shoe stores are the same. Most quick-serve restaurants do what they do in an identical fashion. Most department stores are indistinguishable from one another. This sameness doesn't just happen by chance. It happens systematically over time. Retailers go to the same industry conferences, read the same industry magazines and deal with the same industry suppliers. They abide by the same laws and hire the same consultants. They're all ingesting the same raw materials, and in doing so they all become dangerously similar.

This sameness applies to movie theaters, hotels, banks, shopping centers—you name it. Far from differentiating themselves, competitors within industries actually tend to become more similar over time, which not only leaves them open to commoditization relative to one another but also renders their entire industry open to disruption from the outside. Disruption that we see unfolding around us every day, and often with earth-shattering consequences.

Do you think Ford, GM or Chrysler ever believed that Tesla, a company less than two decades old, would be the one to reimagine how automobiles are to be built, sold and serviced? Or that Gillette ever imagined that the subscription razor blade company Dollar Shave Club would sell $150 million in blades and develop a market value of $1 billion? Do you figure Hilton Hotels ever suspected that Airbnb, a startup that began with one air mattress on a living room floor in San Francisco, would, within seven years of its founding, put more people in more rooms each year than it does?

> "We try to rationalize why innovations
> from other sectors don't apply to us,
> rather than focusing on why they do."
> **GEORGE BLANKENSHIP**

Each of these examples signifies that we have exited the era of business in which success was tied to scale, labor resources, machinery and capital and entered a time in which anyone with a game-changing idea can dramatically alter the course of an entire industry in the blink of an eye.

The lesson in this new era is that the real competition is no longer your known competitors. In fact, the more hardened your gaze becomes on known competition, the bigger your blind spot to disruptors becomes. I tell my clients to think of it this way: assume that right now there's a twenty-four-year-old living in their parents' basement in Palo Alto who's inventing something that will put your company out of business, because there probably is. The question is, can you invent that something first? Can you be the disruptor in your own industry and move light-years ahead of your known competitors? In other words, can you put you out of business before they do?

Setting the Stage
for Innovation

UNDERSTANDING THAT CHANGE is taking place at an exponential pace, we must also appreciate that the comfortable, incremental levels of innovation that were once enough to sustain your business will no longer cut it. The future will belong only to those capable of exponential rates of innovation.

What I've long found interesting, though, is that the very concept of innovation in many companies is often misunderstood, and at best, loosely supported. For example, almost every company I work with claims to prize innovation. They extol it as a corporate virtue and consider it core to their strategy. Most see innovation as inextricably baked into their brand values, and all seem to agree that the antidote to constant disruption is an equally constant level of innovation. In other words, innovation is the shit!

Yet I can easily count on one hand the number of companies that actually invest in identifying, measuring, nurturing or rewarding the human organizational creativity that fuels such innovation. This is particularly ironic because corporations are notorious for measuring even the most inconsequential and tedious of things, yet the vast and astounding value of creativity is most often overlooked or, worse, treated like black magic that simply occurs as spontaneously as lightning strikes. Creativity is undoubtedly one of the least measured and most misunderstood assets a company possesses.

Consequently, while almost all companies aspire to be innovative, remarkably few ever actually are. And should we really be surprised? After all, how can you deploy the right people against innovation initiatives without first understanding who your most creative employees are? How can you expect the organization to adopt innovation as a guiding mantra without nurturing a supportive and adventurous culture? How can you ask people to make time to innovate without rewarding the creativity that sparks it? Clearly you can't, and this is a problem because there may not have been a time in history when innovation was more critical to business success than it is right now.

To give you a better sense of what you're up against, in a recent quarterly report, Amazon listed the "highlights" from the quarter. In all, there were twenty-six separate major initiatives—new products, technologies, programs, content, platforms, alliances and business models. For most companies, twenty-six initiatives would be an ambitious year. At Amazon, it's a typical quarter. Amazon is a veritable innovation factory. So, whoever you are, whatever you sell, if you want to stay in the game, you're going to need to innovate like you've never innovated before. And you need to begin right now. But my guess is, you already sense that.

In fact, so many of the executives I speak to know full well that their company's innovation efforts are falling short but express tremendous frustration at the level of organizational inertia that exists regarding innovation. The hard part, they say, is knowing where to begin in unlocking the creative horsepower required to drive the business forward. With this idea in mind, here are a number of ways to unleash your company's innovativeness.

Start by defining "innovation"

You may feel the meaning of innovation is something organizations should understand intuitively, yet I frequently hear executives talk about "innovative" things their companies are doing that in fact aren't truly innovative. They may be worthy and ambitious initiatives but they're not innovative—and there is a difference. So, what is it precisely? *Webster's* dictionary offers the following simple definitions of innovation:

1. a new idea, device, or method
2. the act or process of introducing new ideas, devices, or methods[1]

It holds, then, that in order for something to be innovative, it first needs to be new or original, something that did not exist previously. However, what executives are very often describing when they talk about what their companies are working on is not *innovation*. It's not entirely new or original but an *iteration* of something that already exists.

For example, though we commonly think of Apple as the innovator of the smartphone, that's not the case. In fact, the first device we could call a smartphone was IBM's 1994 Simon product, which even had a touchscreen. The iPhone, which came along thirteen years later, was a brilliant *iteration* of smartphone technology that included some remarkably innovative features, such as the multi-touch display.

This may sound like nitpicking, but it's vital for organizations to clearly distinguish between "innovation" and "iteration" and to arrive at a commonly accepted internal delineation between the two. For example, Whirlpool believes that for an idea to be truly innovative, it must be "unique and compelling to the consumer, create a competitive advantage, sit on a migration path that can yield further innovations and provide consumers with more value than anything else in the market."[2] For Whirlpool, defining innovation in this way creates a common internal understanding and benchmark for innovative projects. Its use of a common definition also prevents the organization from deceiving itself into believing it's being innovative when it's not—a distinction too many businesses make only when it's too late.

It's also important to distinguish between innovation and iteration because the two are often met with very different reactions, both inside and outside of the organization. Innovation (as much as we all claim to love it) has a proven tendency to make people uncomfortable because it introduces ideas, concepts and products that are new and unfamiliar and challenge people's understanding. Schoolteachers, for example, often consciously promote creativity as a goal of education but frequently display a discomfort with children who seem overly curious and non-conforming—both of which are traits closely associated with creativity.[3] It stands to reason therefore that for many of us, our introduction to creativity was witnessing a classmate being shot down by an authority figure for attempting to be creative. And the experience was even worse when we were the one being shot down!

We carry these aversions and proclivities forward with us into our corporate lives. The work of truly innovative people is often based on developing ideas that create uncertainty and ambiguity, which are two things many businesses don't deal well with. Most companies, executives and boards seek the most certain path forward, a tendency that doesn't bode well for innovation. Innovation is, by definition, a venture into the unknown, a deliberate exercise in uncertainty.

What makes innovation particularly suspect in most corporate environments is that it's very often unsupportable with data. Data, of course, is a mirror on the past and can only tell us about what is known. If something is truly innovative, there is no data available for it. How could there be? It's never existed before. Therefore, any data to support innovation has to be created by the innovator after the fact. This is where iteration comes in.

Iteration can be defined as

a procedure in which repetition of a sequence of operations yields results successively closer to a desired result.[4]

I want to be clear here; iteration is no less valuable than innovation, nor does iteration conflict in any way with innovation. In some cases, iteration can lead to breakthrough innovations. Nonetheless, they are different processes that often prompt very different reactions.

Iteration often gets a gentler ride in organizations because it improves upon things that are already generally accepted, comfortable and familiar. It causes less anxiety and uncertainty and is viewed as less threatening. As a consequence, iteration generally gets more immediate support than innovation. The executive who commits to making the company's existing products even better will likely get full support. The employee who proposes to replace all the company's existing products with an entirely new and unheard of array of items, however, will often be shut out—even if it's the right thing to do.

Until such biases are reconciled, an organization can't successfully move forward. It can't demand innovation but only accept iteration. Therefore, arriving at a common internal definition of both is essential.

Test for creativity

Equally problematic can be operating on the premise that everyone is equally capable of generating innovative ideas. They're not. And to compound the problem, most companies don't even test to discover who their most creative people are.

Organizations routinely test for intelligence quotient (IQ) and emotional quotient (EQ), but exceedingly few ever test employees for their *creativity quotient,* which can be fairly easily measured through a variety of standard tests. The Torrance Tests of Creative Thinking, for example, are one of the more well known.[5] What you'll find is that while we may all start life with similar amounts of creativity, we don't all retain it the same way.

And the ultimate question is, if you expect your finance people to be adept at finance and your legal team to be adept at the law, why on earth wouldn't you expect those charged with innovation to have a proven skill at innovation? Without identifying and inventorying your most creative employees, you're ignoring one of your most valuable organizational assets. Even worse, you may be charging those least capable of producing innovation with the responsibility for it, dooming your efforts from the outset.

Nurture creativity

Interestingly, when you research the idea of nurturing creativity, much of what you turn up are papers and studies having to do with children. Clearly we place significant emphasis on feeding creativity from a young age. There's precious little to be found, however, on how and why creative nurturing is important for adult workers. Somehow we assume that adults don't require the same support, coaching and security to develop and express their creativity.

Much of what we call creativity is better characterized as divergent thinking. Divergent thinkers can examine a situation and develop an array of possible solutions or alternative outcomes. Give a divergent thinker a paper clip and they'll be able to imagine dozens of alternative uses for it. Give a non-divergent thinker the same paper clip and they'll struggle to see it as anything other than what it is. In essence, divergent thinkers can see in a situation what others miss. They can imagine things that others simply can't.

Given the inherent value of divergent thinking, you'd imagine it would be carefully nurtured from a young age. In fact, studies indicate that we systematically drum the divergent thinking out of our children as they get older. According to Sir Ken Robinson, an internationally recognized leader in the development of creativity and education, one such study suggested that "of 1,600 children aged three to five who were tested, 98% showed they could think in divergent ways. By the time they were aged eight to 10, only 32% could think divergently. When the same test was applied to 13 to 15-year-olds, only 10% could think in this way. And when the test was used with 200,000 25-year-olds, only 2% could think divergently."[6] Only 2 percent!

In the corporate environment, then, we not only have to encourage creativity, we have to invest in supporting its *redevelopment* in the people who work for and with us. We have to train people to once again think divergently. Once we've identified them in the organization, these highly creative minds must be supported and nurtured.

If you believe that creativity happens by sticking a group of people in a conference room with a pot of coffee and a flip chart, you're going to be sadly disappointed. Google's Jonathan Rosenberg once said, "Creativity can be allocated, it can be budgeted, it can be measured, it can be tracked and encouraged but it can't be dictated."[7] In other words, creativity cannot be commanded; rather, it must be cajoled into taking flight. Creativity doesn't come from a tap that you turn on when you need it. With the right climate, conditions and working methods, however, it can flow more freely and steadily throughout your company.

Allowing employees to work on passion projects is one means of liberating their creativity. Giving people the freedom to learn new skills, work in different surroundings, either with other people or alone (if that suits their creative process better), can all support greater levels of creativity and innovation. Creativity thrives on variety and constant stimulus.

Reward creativity

Most corporate reward systems are biased toward success, and that's a problem when it comes to innovation because many of the most innovative ideas are not immediately successful in a conventional business sense. They may not produce instant gains in sales, profit, customer satisfaction or market share. In fact, they may simply cost the company money. However, that doesn't mean they're not valuable or don't help to evolve organizational strategy. Therefore, rewarding creativity means evaluating innovation on its own merits and celebrating the controlled but instructive failure that often accompanies it. This is not to imply that success isn't the ultimate goal, but by tilting a company's reward and recognition system solely toward success, organizations run the risk of stifling the innovations necessary to achieve it. When people are walking a tightrope of success with their annual bonus at the other end, they're a lot less likely to risk falling!

You can talk about innovation, you can wish for innovation, but until you identify your most creative employees and give them the supportive culture and conditions in which to innovate, you'll get nowhere. Only after you've begun to identify, nurture and reward creativity will you begin to see its spoils. And if you're like most organizations, chances are you're sitting on a gold mine.

Cultivating an
Innovative Mindset

ONCE YOU'VE IDENTIFIED the key creative people in your organization and created an environment that sets them up for success, how do you move forward with the sometimes daunting task of innovating? One of the best ways is to cultivate an innovative mindset by encouraging employees to question everything.

The power of *what if*

When you trace disruptive businesses back to their moment of inception, many began with a what-if moment. Reed Hastings asked, what if movies could come to you instead of you going to a video store? Netflix was born. Travis Kalanick and Garrett Camp asked, what if you could solve the problem of getting a cab in San Francisco anytime you needed one? Now people in San Francisco and hundreds of other cities use Uber. Neil Blumenthal asked, what if glasses could be sold online? Today, Warby Parker is valued at more than a billion dollars.

What if are the two most powerful words on Earth. And yet, in many companies they're rarely spoken. The obstacle for most organizations is the tyranny of practicality and pragmatism. They discourage employees from dreaming big in favor of doing what's possible, feasible and manageable. Those who muddy discussions with "what ifs" are regarded as dreamers and nuisances, getting in the way of what needs to get done with limited resources. They ultimately get drowned out by the "voices of reason."

The other problem is that our business culture favors ideas and answers over questions. We have plenty of brainstorming sessions aimed at solving business problems, but when was the last time you attended a what-if session aimed at opening up possibilities? Regrettably, many leaders tend to discriminate against what-if questions and treat them as fanciful, pie-in-the-sky notions. And that has to change in order for companies to alter their course, according to Warren Berger, author of *A More Beautiful Question*. "Leaders can also encourage companywide questioning by being more curious and inquisitive themselves," he says. He cautions, however: "This is not necessarily easy for senior executives, who are used to being the ones with the answers."[1] Unfortunately, the act of questioning, particularly in Western business culture, is very often construed as weakness, when in fact it's one of the clearest indications of intellectual strength.

So how do you build a *what-if* culture? An important first step may be to identify the loudest voices of reason in the company—those who carry buckets of cold water with them into every meeting—then, fire them and replace them with dreamers.

The power of *why not*

Equally important to asking *what if*, is questioning *why not*. Asking why not is a crucial means of addressing the paradigms and limitations that most companies simply come to accept.

These electrified third rails that businesses are told never, ever to touch—industry norms, legislative barriers, perceived customer preferences, political boundaries or cultural sensibilities—are all elements that can hamstring companies into looking just like their competitors, and they are therefore precisely the things that newcomers to an industry attack. They're not afraid to ask why not.

Pirch attacked the idea that a kitchen, bath and outdoor store needed to look and act like a warehouse. TOMS challenged the idea that a retail space couldn't be a place where loitering turned into revenue. And STORY and b8ta dispelled the centuries-old notion that retail success must be tied to product sales. Simply asking why not can be the catalyst for epic creative breakthroughs.

Change the script

Ask "what if" and "why not" enough and they will lead you to do things differently, and even small differences in your customer experience, relative to industry norms, can make a dramatic difference.

To the point, I recently came across an interesting study compiled by five researchers from Santa Clara University who set out to validate a phenomenon known as the Pique Technique. When used in certain situations, this technique can increase our agreeability to requests when our reflexive reaction would otherwise be refusal.[2]

In one example, researchers posed as panhandlers. One group used an approach typical to most panhandlers by simply asking if people passing by could "spare some change." Another group took a different approach, asking for specific and unusual amounts such as twenty-seven cents, which would no doubt strike passersby as unusual. As it turned out, the study showed that passersby consistently gave more money, more often, to the panhandlers who asked for unusual amounts.

The researchers concluded that, as humans, we develop a script in our mind of how a certain situation is likely to play out and we become predisposed to a response, and it's often a negative one. But if that script is broken in our mind, we immediately become more inclined to be compliant or approving. In other words, when people in the study saw the panhandler, the script in their mind might have read:

Panhandler: Excuse me, can you spare some change?
Passerby: Sorry, I don't have any change on me.

However, when the panhandler asked for an unusual amount of money, the "refusal script" was broken and the attention of the passerby was, quite beyond their control, piqued. In this state, more of them complied with the request.

I find this result fascinating because we go into so many situations with a script prewritten in our minds. When we enter a restaurant, bank online or go to a store, we carry a script of what that experience will be. For example, when I visit a restaurant, I expect to be greeted by a host or hostess, asked how many there are in my party and walked to my table. A short time thereafter, I assume a waiter or busperson will arrive to pour water and ask if I'd like anything else to drink—a glass of wine, perhaps. Moments later, I expect the waiter will return to take my order and soon after my food will arrive. I will eat, be asked if I'd like dessert and coffee and the check will follow. End of experience, end of script, fade to black.

But what if we could change elements of that script? What if I could order and pay for my entire meal before I arrived at the restaurant? What if, instead of a human host, a robot greeted and escorted me to my table? What if, instead of bringing me the check, the waiter brought me a very small gift or token expression of thanks? How might this change of script alter my experience and willingness to spend and, ultimately, increase my level of joy with the experience?

When it comes to retail, consumers have well-formed scripts. When entering a store, we anticipate that a clerk will ask, "Can I help you?" When we check out, we expect the cashier to ask, "Did you find everything you were looking for?" As a consequence, we respond reflexively, according to the script. I've even found myself telling salespeople "I'm just looking" purely out of instinct, even when I could actually use their help.

Breakthroughs can occur once we identify the typical script in our industry or category. Once we understand what consumers are preprogrammed to expect, we can then look for creative, relevant and valuable ways to change the script to create surprise, interest and infinitely more unique experiences.

Consider the way a company like Uber changed the script in our mind about how we hire a taxi. The entire experience, from the moment I contact the driver to the time I pay for the ride, is a complete departure from the experience we've been conditioned by the taxi industry to expect. By introducing new and unexpected scripting, Uber immediately captured the public's attention and scaled an enormous user base.

Produce prototypes, not just ideas

All too often, companies view innovation as a process aimed at generating ideas. While this is partly true, if the only output of the creative process is ideas, the effort will likely end in frustration. No doubt you've attended brainstorming sessions that end with an armload of scrawled-upon flip chart paper getting hauled back to an office and transcribed into a meeting memory document that ultimately dies a quiet death because no one ever looks at it again.

> "The speed of innovation is so fast today that even companies which embrace transformative innovation are finding that the pace of change, rather than being incremental, is far more rapid than they could ever have imagined." LUCIE GREENE

The reason isn't because there aren't good ideas in there. It's often because the lag time between the idea and the intended execution is so long that the ideas lose energy and competing work creeps in to obviate them from the organizational priority list. This approach kills innovation in two ways: first, you don't benefit from the ideas generated, and second, creators in your organization lose faith in the creative process. If all this innovation never moves to execution, why even bother?

Instead, your innovation teams should work to prototype the best ideas almost immediately—not in weeks or months but within hours or days, if possible. At Google, staff use what they call a Design Sprint process that unfolds over a five-day period and has an equivalent number of steps. Using these steps, groups can go from ideation to testing in a fraction of the time normally attributed to innovation cycles. The steps are

→ **Unpack.** Bring in all required people and all available information to define the goal of the innovation session and download everything required to inform the team's work. Be extremely clear about what the purpose of the session is. Include all relevant people, data and insights.
→ **Sketch.** Have individuals (not groups) create detailed sketches of their solutions to the problem or opportunity.

→ **Decide.** Using a standardized set of criteria drawn from the goals of the session, get the group to assess each sketched solution and decide on the one(s) to take to prototype.

→ **Prototype.** Quickly mock up, build or otherwise create a representation of the solution that can be tested.

→ **Test.** Put the solution in front of twenty potential consumers, allowing them to try it and capturing their individual responses, feeling and thoughts.

If you can build the organizational discipline to create prototypes, not just ideas, you will not only out-innovate the competitor you know, you just might stave off the competitor you don't know. In the end, those who own the future will not only have great ideas but they will be the fastest to make their great ideas a reality.

Go first

Any business that is perfectly comfortable with its long-term strategy likely won't exist in ten years. I say that because if an organization is truly innovating, it will inevitably be developing ideas and concepts that seem inherently disruptive, risky or downright crazy. Frankly, if your strategy doesn't make you a little queasy, it's probably not that innovative. In fact, it's probably a carbon copy of what your competitors are comfortably developing!

Any race car driver will tell you that the only way to win races consistently is to drive at what is referred to as *the ragged edge*—the razor-thin space between full control and absolute calamity. To drive at this pace means keeping one's foot pressed to the accelerator when others lose their nerve and lift it off. Similarly, your company has to be prepared to act on compelling, unconventional and unproven concepts to move your business to the ragged edge, so to speak, of innovation.

This approach doesn't necessarily mean being the first to launch; rather, it means being the first to wonder, the first to explore, to test, to learn and, yes, when something looks like a winner, the first to jump in with both feet.

> ## "Don't fear mistakes.
> ## There are none."
> **MILES DAVIS**

The key to developing the organizational courage to go first lies in developing a system and structure for innovation—an accepted manner of scanning the landscape for ideas and moving them into testing, evaluation and execution.

As early as 2009, for example, Starbucks began testing mobile payment in a small sixteen-store trial in the Seattle area. Far from betting the farm on mobile, the company tested the technology in parallel with its existing and highly successful loyalty card program. By 2011, after significant learning, Starbucks fully rolled out its mobile payment and within nine weeks had processed 3 million mobile transactions. Within a year, the number had reached 26 million.[3] Today, upwards of a quarter of all payments at Starbucks are made using the app, making the company a leader in the mobile payments arena and leaving most other retailers scratching their heads.

One can pore over the finer points of how Starbucks managed to achieve this result, but two things are clear: the company displayed an early curiosity and willingness to test mobile and, when the potential for mobile became relatively clear, it was unafraid to pull the trigger and invest substantially.

Similarly, your business, whatever it is, must remain curious and willing to venture into the unknown, albeit in a safe way. You also need to be prepared to invest where your curiosity leads to obvious opportunity. *Could have, should have* and *would have* are the epitaphs of business that failed to act.

In instances when your testing comes up empty or your curiosity proves unfounded, you (not your competitors) will benefit from the learning and insight that such efforts avail. You will carry that intelligence forward.

Implementing
Innovation

I RECEIVE A tremendous amount of marketing communication through my preferred airline's loyalty program: invitations for discounted travel, information on new offers, popular destinations and any number of other things. I can't be sure what it costs the airline to maintain these communications but I suspect when we multiply it by the number of customers who receive the same messaging, it's got to be significant.

On a recent flight, after boarding and taking my seat, I looked to my left and found that the window next to me had a thick layer of duct tape installed completely around its perimeter, as though holding the window in place. Now, I'm not an engineer, and to be honest I didn't do all that well in high school physics, but something about a duct-taped window in an aircraft didn't make me exceedingly comfortable. In the end, I quelled any thoughts of impending disaster with an Ativan and hoped for the best. I'll save you any suspense... I survived.

But the duct-taped window got me thinking. Here was an airline spending all this money to target me with promotions, offers and discounts, pleading for more business and loyalty. And yet, all the while, that window was allowed to remain duct-taped together, making a very clear statement to every passenger that happened to see it, or worse yet, sit beside it like I did.

This airline is really no different than most other companies. We all have aspects of our businesses that must appear to our customers to be duct-taped together. We all have things in our businesses that are broken and that we willingly turn a blind eye to. We convince ourselves that no one will notice and that eventually we'll get around to fixing the problems. Unfortunately, we get so used to seeing the problems that we become blind to them, and, to us at least, they cease to exist. In the meantime, however, we've left the door (or the broken window as it were) open to our competitors.

For example, in January of 2015, a major U.S. retailer filed a patent aimed at completely reinventing the in-store shopping and payment experience. The patent document described a system whereby shoppers would be able to enter the store, select the items they wish to buy and leave. No checkouts. No cashiers. No waiting. The shopper would simply leave with the items and have them automatically charged to their preferred method of payment. To pull this off, the company described an elaborate system of video analytics, radio frequency identification tags and readers, sensors and processors—all aimed at speeding shoppers in and out of the store without friction.

Now, you might be thinking that this patent was probably the work of a major retailer. After all, it would make sense for a Nordstrom, Tesco, Target or Walmart—all of which would be intimately familiar with the frustrations that checkout lines cause—to be innovating wildly to do away with them, right? Unfortunately, you'd be wrong. This patent was filed by their archenemy, Amazon—which less than a year later would announce its concrete plans to launch Amazon Go, an

1800-square-foot grocery and convenience store concept, devoid of any checkout lines or cashiers. Just as Amazon had suggested in its patent filing, shoppers would simply scan their mobile device upon entering, collect the products they wanted and walk out. Legalized shoplifting, if you will. Upon word of the announcement, you could almost hear a collective "holy shit" come from the grocery industry.

You see, to conventional retailers, the inconvenience of the checkout process has become a duct-taped window that they are now oblivious to. The archaic nature of the process escapes them. It clearly doesn't escape Amazon, however. To Amazon, checkout lines are only one of many broken windows in retail— just one of the known friction points that retailers force their customers to live with, representing yet another opportunity for innovation. Fixing the duct-taped windows within your own organization can be a great starting point for your innovation journey.

Make it ten times better

That Amazon didn't just propose to make the retail checkout process better but looked to do away with it entirely is an example of what Astro Teller, head of Google's X division, deems a "moonshot"—a project or proposal that improves something by ten times versus 10 percent. Most businesses, he points out, attempt to improve things by 10 percent. They work on existing assumptions, build on existing models and extend existing resources. And most often these attempts get bogged down and lose energy. If the prize is only 10 percent better than the current reality, it's easy to see why people might lose interest; but if the goal is to be ten times better than the status quo, that's an entirely more engaging prospect.

For example, the struggling greeting card and gift industry has been swimming against a tide of change. The entire nature of how we celebrate, recognize and commemorate occasions has changed entirely. In response, some major greeting card incumbents have attempted to improve their prospects by adding selections of gift items and electronic cards, and enabling the personalization of greeting cards and gifts. While I respect the initiative, the problem is that all of these noble efforts are attempted 10 percent improvements. They all begin with two going-in assumptions: first, that cards and gifts are how people express occasions and sentiments; and second, that they are a greeting *card* company. What, I wonder, might happen if they instead attempted a ten-times leap and reimagined the entire concept of how we celebrate occasions? Could you send a hologram of yourself to a relative on their birthday? Could you use VR so you can actually *be* with a sick loved one on the other side of the planet or attend a wedding, birthday party or other celebration? Could Hallmark reinvent the party planning industry? Could greeting card companies align with a travel company to create spectacular "occasion travel," opportunities for people to celebrate together in exotic places? Could all the energy, money and time that's going into trying to salvage a dying category be redeployed to invent new categories entirely?

> "Once we rid ourselves of
> traditional thinking, we can get on with
> creating the future." JAMES BERTRAND

Improving something by ten times, Teller argues, is actually easier than improving it by 10 percent: "When you aim for a 10× gain, you lean instead on bravery and creativity—the kind that, literally and metaphorically, can put a man on the moon. That's what 10× does that 10 percent could never do. 10× can light a fire in hearts, and it's hard not to get excited and think that other, seemingly impossible things might also be possible. And that, counter-intuitively, makes the hardest things much easier to accomplish than you might think."[1]

As we look to the future of retail, how can we apply Teller's 10× principle to the customer experience? How can we ensure that we innovate to a place that is not merely incrementally better than what we have today but an exponential improvement?

Start with free

An interesting way to break the organizational tendency to innovate by 10 percent and move toward ten-times improvement is to imagine a future state in which the product(s) you sell will be free or sold to customers at cost. In that future, how could your business survive? How could you still generate revenue? What other business models or revenue streams could be introduced to make up the shortfall? What value could you offer customers over and above the product itself?

Starting with free is an important exercise for a couple of reasons. First, it might actually become the case. Consider that in many verticals we may soon reach a point at which the available profit between wholesale and retail is nil. If that sounds like I'm simply shouting "fire" in a movie theater, it's worth taking a look at where retail profit margins are headed. Retailers from New York to Melbourne have been doggedly battling declining profits. Tesco's 2015 annual financial report, for example, cited a trading margin of +/- 1.07 percent. That's about as close as you can come to zero without actually being there. And as long as Amazon, through its AmazonFresh business, is willing to sell products at a loss in order to acquire customers, the reality is that Tesco and many other businesses may soon be confronted with the prospect of being taken underwater.

Second, by starting from the assumption that your product is free, you will force your organization to think more laterally about what you do. You'll explore ideas, services and concepts that may seem more tangential or peripheral but may indeed add significant value to the experience your customers enjoy.

The question is simply, how else could your retail business make money? Could you create experiences that are so good that customers are willing to pay for them? Would shoppers pay to become members? Could you hold instructional events in your space that are so fantastic that shoppers would happily pay admission? Could you showcase products that are difficult to find—prototypes and concept products? Or could your store be an experiential laboratory, a real-world research facility, a data factory that brands are willing to pay to access and learn from?

Instead of aisles of cans and boxes, could the grocery space of the future feature chefs, nutritional consultants, cooking classes and health care facilities? Could the entire look and merchandising of the store change monthly to feature a new cultural culinary landscape? Could you use the space to create spectacle and theater? Would brands pay to be a part of it, either by hosting classes and events or being part of celebrity chef demonstrations?

Unfortunately, too many businesses forestall this kind of wide-open scenario planning until it's too late—until they have no choice but to innovate but, because the business is so badly war-torn, have neither the funding nor the talent left to do so.

Think like an insurgent

It may come as little surprise that, despite the ambitious growth projections of most business leaders, the majority of businesses fail to outgrow their markets. In fact, according to Bain & Company, the number of businesses that lag behind the average growth rate in their market is roughly 90 percent. And of incumbent companies that fail to meet their growth objectives, only a small number (approximately 15 percent)[2] cite market factors as the cause. The other 85 percent point to internal causes such as organizational complexity, weaknesses in corporate culture and the inability to focus their efforts.

The answer, according to Bain & Company's James Allen, is to recapture what he calls the Founder's Mentality—an absolute clarity of vision and focus that can reinvigorate a company's performance. Doing so, however, often means unwinding decades of the bureaucracy and inertia that come with growth and scale.

Founder-led companies, Allen points out, tend to be market insurgents with an intense focus on the needs of the customer, a bias toward action and a focus on frontline talent and strategy. Unfortunately, insurgents, as you would expect, can become seduced by the benefits of scale and scope. Scale allows for better organizational economics—you can buy more advantageously. Scope allows your company to enter new markets or categories. All of this, of course, looks very attractive, and as a result, insurgents grow to become incumbents.

For a while, incumbents enjoy the benefits that their greater size affords them. The problem occurs, however, when the by-products of scale and scope become impediments to growth and actually dilute organizational focus and action. Eventually the drawbacks of being a large incumbent outweigh the benefits, and organizations begin to lose—often without knowing precisely why.

Many forces can push an insurgent company off its path, but in my opinion, the most insidious of them is market pressure to grow at all costs, purely to satisfy investor greed. For example, clothing retailer Lululemon Athletica, which was founded in 1998, arrived in the market as an insurgent brand focused on yoga-inspired apparel. The company rapidly became known for its unique store environments, remarkable service, outstanding design and quality—and also for the quirky and, yes, sometimes downright bizarre and polarizing leadership of its founder, Chip

Wilson. Bottom line... it was a company with a very keen mission and focus on its customers.

In the early years, the company grew slowly and steadily, posting strong same-store performance. However, in 2007, Wilson decided to take the company public, and beginning in 2008, Lululemon started on a growth tear that would see its store count more than triple within five years. Scale and scope became its strategy. As the chain grew, however, other problems arose. Same-store sales performance became erratic and ultimately dropped to near 0 percent, and catastrophic product-quality issues arose. The company that practically invented the yoga apparel category had a substantially weakened brand and was surrounded by competition.

This tendency to make growth a strategy is something that Starbucks CEO Howard Schultz is all too familiar with. "When you look at growth as a strategy," he has said, "it becomes somewhat seductive, addictive. But growth... is not a strategy; it's a tactic."[3] Following an eight-year hiatus as Starbucks chairman, Schultz was reinstated as CEO after the company's sales and stock performance swooned. Between 2000 and 2008, the company had grown from five thousand stores to an astonishing fifteen thousand!

On his return, Schultz saw that a high percentage of stores were failing—many of which had been open less than eighteen months. Moreover, Schultz saw that in its quest for growth, the company had migrated from its attention to quality and customer experience. The decision to open many of the stores during that eight-year period, he realized, was the result of decision-making that was "complicit in the stock price.... You don't want to start making decisions that are based on a PE [price earnings] or a stock price," he said. "We started making decisions that were driving incremental revenue and perhaps were not consistent with the equity of the brand."[4]

In the end, Schultz opted to close more than nine hundred stores and double-down on training, standards and customer experience. It was a return to the "founder's mentality" and an insurgent organizational mindset that helped Schultz and Starbucks pull the nose up on the company's performance, avoiding what many foresaw as certain disaster. This is a clear illustration of why it's vitally important that every organization, particularly large incumbents, maintains a founder's mentality and does whatever is necessary to think like an insurgent.

Here's what I interpret the differences to be between the two mindsets:

INCUMBENT MENTALITY	FOUNDER'S MENTALITY
The company's mission is vaguely and unevenly understood through the organization.	The company has a bold and commonly understood sense of noble purpose, culture and mission.
Is bureaucratic and bogged down by rules, procedures and corporate red tape.	Challenges the status quo and industry paradigms to create disruptive customer value and differentiated experience.
Power in the company flows into the middle, often to people most disconnected from customer needs.	Obsession with the needs of the customer pushes power to the frontline. Staff are empowered to act in the customers' interests.
A bias toward iteration and experimentation but with a lack of decisive action.	A bias toward acting on advantageous innovations quickly and decisively.
Vague and convoluted accountability and greater focus on organizational activities than direct customer needs.	High degree of direct accountability and customer satisfaction.

Unlike incumbents in a market, insurgents tend to have a clear mission and purpose. They attack closely held industry paradigms and sometimes skirt the "rules" in order to deliver more profoundly on perceived customer needs. Uber, for example, challenged the rules and beliefs of the transportation industry to deliver a new and superior customer experience. Netflix challenged paradigms in the video rental industry to create an entirely new way of accessing entertainment. Warby Parker questioned the conventions surrounding how people order prescription eyewear and developed a completely new model.

Don't fall into the technology trap

When you drive your car to work, are you enjoying a combustion-engine propulsion experience or simply riding in your car? When you do your laundry, are you reveling in a hydro-electrically agitated emulsification experience or just cleaning your clothes? When you watch TV, is that a light-emitting diode transmission experience or just entertainment? Posed this way, these questions seem clearly rhetorical. It's pretty obvious in each case that technology is not the experience but merely the platform upon which the experience is delivered. In other words, these are not "technological" experiences. They are simply experiences that incorporate technology.

Yet each day, I speak with, read about or hear of brands and retailers setting out with the sole intent of creating "digital experiences" for their customers. Many have gone so far as to establish in-house labs with the express intent of pumping out digital experiences like they're link sausages. Most of these efforts are loosely aimed at awkwardly injecting a piece of technology into customer interactions. A recent survey of CEOs confirms a sort of digital preoccupation, with respondents rating everything from mobile technologies to the Internet of Things as being "strategically important" to their businesses. Regrettably, I can assure you that a far smaller percentage of CEOs fully understand what many of these technologies are. Nonetheless, digital experiences seem to be de rigueur in business today. Ironically, I believe it's exactly this misplaced digital importance that is causing so many retail innovation efforts to fall flat.

The fact is that no one needs a digital experience at all. What retailers should be setting out to do is to design unique, memorable, valuable experiences—*some of which* may be supported or enabled through digital technologies. Rather than treating the absence of digital as the problem, retail leaders should instead address the absence of remarkable experiences in most of their stores—which to some extent may be aided by incorporating digital solutions. It may sound like mere semantics, but in fact it's a critical distinction that's central to building a meaningful customer experience strategy. In other words, the starting point is not to go digital but to design better experiences.

> "We see a lot of clients get fixated on specific technologies and approaches, but the truth is, nobody pays to see technology, they pay for an experience." **DARREN DAVID AND NATHAN MOODY**

Great retail companies should be approaching their customer experience as a powerful, live enactment of their unique brand story. They need to break their story into a series of moments of truth and then painstakingly apply brilliant design intent to each small but critical customer interaction.

Entering the store, browsing selections, learning and trialing products, receiving service, paying, arranging shipping, exiting the store and even providing after-sale support are all critical turning points in the brand story that must be meticulously

considered and elegantly designed to be deliberate and delightful. Once that unique brand experience is fully imagined,
then, and only then, can decisions be made as to how it could
or should be animated. Some of these experiences may be best
delivered digitally, some may not and still others may come to
life through some combination of digital and nondigital assets.
As former Apple CEO Steve Jobs put it, "You've got to start with
the customer experience and work back to the technology."[5]

So, while I'm an evangelical proponent of leveraging digital
wherever it makes sense and wherever it adds demonstrative
value, I'm an even greater believer that digital for digital's sake is
a road to nowhere. Whether you touch your customers through
the use of technology or not, what really matters is that the
unique brand experience they enjoy is so utterly remarkable that
they long to do it again and again and will share their experience
with anyone who will listen.

This doesn't mean that you shouldn't allow technologies to
catch your eye. They will, and there's nothing wrong with that.
But the key thing is that if a technology doesn't either alleviate
experiential friction or add experiential value for your customers, it's simply not worth considering. Frankly, the world really
doesn't need another app, beacon, push notification or RFID
tag. What it needs are jaw-dropping experiences distilled from
remarkable brand stories and brought to life with brilliant com-
binations of art, science and humanity.

Reengineering Retail

$$\cdot\,\cdot\,\cdot\,\times\,\cdot\,\cdot\,\cdot$$

ONCE YOU'VE LAID the groundwork for a culture of innovation and insurgent thinking, the challenge becomes to actually use those attributes to chart a course forward. The question is how.

When I consider the most powerful lessons I've learned from researching highly innovative and disruptive businesses, three things really stand out. Three things that these businesses tend to do that many of their competitors do not.

They build networks, they benchmark laterally and they engineer everything.

Build networks, not empires

The problems facing retail industry incumbents such as Macy's, Walmart, Best Buy, Tesco and others have less to do with a failure to master omnichannel retailing, harness big data analytics or conquer mobile commerce and much more to do with their core operating structure. They are struggling, in large part, because the very business structure that once made them so powerful now renders them slow-moving targets, ripe for eradication.

These businesses, and others like them, are *empires* built in an era when becoming an empire was the only sure path to strength, power and competitive dominance. They are products of an age when to be successful as an organization was to be inherently monolithic, omnipotent and isolated; an age when cornering a market was only possible after massive capital investment, marketing spend and infrastructure development. The strangleholds these empires achieved in their categories made them darlings of the investment community. In fact, famed investor Warren Buffett has often noticeably sought out and invested in companies that he believes have what he terms the "widest competitive moat" around them: island empires reigning supreme in their markets.

In the pre-digital era, Buffett's strategy made perfect sense. Innovation moved at an industrial pace and corporate scale was tied more directly to capital: machinery, people, real estate and infrastructure. In the post-digital era, however, business empires are steadily giving up ground to *networks*. In a post-digital landscape, innovation now moves at an exponential pace, and scale is achievable without the trappings of bureaucracy. Uber is a mere seven years old and operates in more than five hundred cities worldwide, yet it doesn't own a single taxi or limousine. Moreover, because Uber is really nothing more than an operating platform, it's nimble enough to shape-shift easily from livery company to food delivery company with the addition of the simple suffix "eats" to its name. In essence, Uber can become whatever it wants to become, without the need for massive additional capital investment or corporate infrastructure.

> "Facebook is quite entrenched and has a network effect. It's hard to break into a network once it's formed." **ELON MUSK**

This same level of rapid scaling applies to retail networks. Whereas Walmart has sixty thousand suppliers, its supply chain is dwarfed by networked rival Etsy, which has an astonishing 850,000 vendor partners. It's becoming abundantly clear that networks eat empires for breakfast.

Furthermore, because empires are closed systems, they often, quite naturally, place the well-being of the empire above all other stakeholders, frequently resulting in revolt from shareholders, friction with suppliers, grievances with employees and disloyalty from customers.

Because they tend to be more insular and secretive in their innovation efforts, empires also tend to adapt to changing consumer and market dynamics at a glacial rate, putting themselves at risk of falling well behind innovation cycles.

And lastly, so much organizational energy goes into simply sustaining the empires themselves that it depletes energy that could be spent focusing on customers—and that is precisely what most often precipitates their eventual demise.

Networks, on the other hand, are capital-light, structurally lean and able to scale rapidly. They operate on transparency and a sense of shared ownership with peer-to-peer trust and governance. Their success ultimately depends on a balanced scorecard of stakeholder interests, from shareholders to employees and network partners. They are more fluid, flexible and adaptable to change, in large part because they offer an intrinsically broader collective market intelligence. And because networks are often a gathering of "long-tail" products and services, they can provide more interesting, niche and often higher-margin items than empire businesses, which have a greater need to appeal to mass tastes and preferences with commodity products. Most importantly, because networks have less infrastructure than empire businesses, all members of the network can dedicate more of their energy to delighting customers, thus creating a virtuous cycle that returns value to the network as a whole.

The successful retailer of the future, therefore, will build its business not as a walled fortress with a deep moat but more like an open application program—a proliferative platform that others can plug into and flourish, allowing the network and all of its members to succeed.

Benchmark laterally

It's natural in any industry to compare one's company, strategy and performance almost exclusively to competitors within the category or sector. Decades ago, this type of comparison was not only common but also a viable competitive approach. Today, it's one of the most potentially deadly things a company can fall prey to doing.

By way of example, have you ever met anyone who really loves their cable company? Me neither. In fact, most of us reserve a special level of disdain for our cable provider. Between service outages, confusing pricing structures, lackluster customer support and long lead times for repairs, what is there to love? On the other hand, having advised cable companies in the past, I can tell you that the people who work for them are largely good people who work just as hard at their jobs as you and I do. They are bright businesspeople who understand what's going on and their goal is to make customers happy. Given this, how is it that so few of us have any affection for our cable company?

The problem lies in how cable companies benchmark their businesses. They seem to believe that if they can achieve a level of performance slightly less horrible than that of other cable companies, they will appear awesome by comparison. They don't aspire to be great; they only aim to be incrementally better than their known competition. In a world where other cable companies were the only competition, this approach could suffice. And in a pre-digital world, where choices were limited and disruption was rare, consumers had little choice but to measure the performance of their cable company in the same way—not good, but a little better than the other guys.

In a post-digital world, however, where disruption is routine and options are abundant, consumers take a different view. We're no longer simply comparing one cable company to another. We're wondering why Netflix costs $9.99 per month but cable can cost more than a hundred. Moreover, we're curious as to why a Tesla automobile can be serviced while we sleep, but our cable modems can't be repaired in the same way. If we get great, personalized service at a Marriott hotel when we spend just one night, why can't we get similarly pleasant service from our cable company when we pay it thousands of dollars per year? And if we can use our mobile devices to hail an Uber taxi, know the name of the driver who will be picking us up and literally watch its route as it makes its way to us, why is the cable company still giving us an eight-hour window for a service call, and forcing us to stay home from work for an entire day? Why?!

Increasingly, the chasm between what we know is possible and what we get from such empire-based companies is gaping. The result of this experiential dissonance is that *all* cable companies suddenly leave themselves wide open to disruption from market alternatives such as Netflix, Apple and Amazon. And once the damage is done, customers can migrate so quickly they're gone forever. There is no time to backpedal and make up for the past.

Consumers are now benchmarking their experiences laterally, and retailers must benchmark their performance accordingly. It's no longer good enough for department store A to be a little better than department store B. That only means that department store A will declare bankruptcy a little later than B. Instead, the question for department store A should be, how good is it compared to experiences offered by, say, Etsy, Spotify, Walt Disney World or Virgin Airlines? That's how good every business now needs to be.

Therefore, it's essential that retailers constantly scan the horizon for the trends and technologies that are fundamentally shifting consumer behaviors and incorporate those learnings into their businesses. As authors Gary Hamel and Nancy Tennant wrote recently, "To be an innovator, you don't need a crystal ball: you need a wide-angle lens. You have to be tracking trends your competitors haven't yet noticed, then figuring out ways of using them to upend traditional business models."[1]

Only through aggressive lateral benchmarking can your business stay ahead of consumer behavior.

Engineer everything

I reckon that if you and I were to visit ten local stores together today, the experiences that we'd have in at least eight of them would be largely accidental. What I mean is that whether the experience was positive or negative, it would largely depend on circumstance, coincidence and chance and not on any deliberate or carefully planned experiential design. Whoever happened to be working that day, what mood they were in, what they happened to say to us when we arrived and ultimately how they met our needs would, more often than not, be entirely unplanned.

I've always found this curious. After all, most companies will agonize over the smallest details when it comes to things such as the taglines, logo colors and typefaces used in ads, yet exceptionally few apply as much concern or discipline to their customer experience. In fact, in a world where businesses monitor, measure and micromanage just about every other aspect of their enterprises, the degree to which we allow customer experience to manage itself is simply unfathomable to me.

Like a stage play without a script, many businesses simply throw the curtain open each day and let the actors ad-lib as best they can. Most satisfy themselves with only a vague notion of the quality of experience being delivered to their customers.

What is abundantly clear from my research, however, is that the best, most successful and future-facing companies obsess about their customer experience above all else. They go to extraordinary lengths to ensure that it's remarkable. And, like the team at Rolex when it's crafting a fine watch, they design, engineer and fine-tune every aspect of it.

Shaun Smith, co-author of the book *On Purpose*, believes that most organizations have customer experience completely backward. "Most organisations," he says, "are very 'loose' when it comes to what their brand stands for and the kind of experience they wish customers to have, but very 'tight' when it comes to telling employees how to behave. Brands that deliver great experiences usually reverse these two, being very 'tight' about what the brand stands for and the experience they wish to create but quite 'loose' in allowing their people freedom in how they satisfy their customers."[2]

Not coincidentally, much of what Smith describes can be attributed to the Founder's Mentality and the innate sense of purpose that pervades highly entrepreneurial organizations. For example, I began my career in retail working for a successful family business where it was common for the seventy-year-old founder to drop into stores and serve customers himself. In fact, he delighted in it. No employee handbook or training program could have had as much impact on his employees as those visits. The positioning of the brand, the expectation of personal performance and the precise and exceptional experience the company aspired to deliver to its customers were all on display every time he arrived at the store.

Of course, it's easy to create that kind of cohesive sense of purpose and brand expectation in a small- or medium-sized company with an abundance of entrepreneurial energy. But how does one create the same tight brand and customer experience expectations at scale? It's clearly a bigger task. Fortunately, it's no less achievable; but it does require thoughtful and deliberate attention to five key experiential elements. Remarkable experiences are

→ **engaging.** They connect to all five senses: of sight, sound, smell, taste and touch. They involve the customer in a visceral way.
→ **unique.** They incorporate methods, language or customs that are unusual, surprising or proprietary but also authentic and natural.
→ **personalized.** The customer feels that the experience they received was somehow just for them.
→ **surprising.** They incorporate elements or interactions that are completely unexpected.
→ **repeatable.** They are executed using prescriptive and tested methods to achieve a uniform level of consistency and excellence across the enterprise.

Individually, any of these five experiential attributes can be achieved by most businesses some of the time. However, very few brands are proficient at consistently delivering experiences incorporating all five, all of the time. The Ritz-Carlton Hotel Company is among the very few enterprises that do, a consequence of both meticulous experiential design and obsessive attention to executional standards; it engineers everything.

Each Ritz-Carlton property is designed with a "scenography," an idea adopted from the thinking of Michael Eagan, a Canadian theater designer and former professor at Canada's National

Theatre School. Eagan defined scenography as "all of the elements that contribute to establishing an atmosphere and mood for a theatrical presentation: lighting, sound, set and costume design."[3] Far from being about clean sheets and room upgrades, Ritz-Carlton works to make each of its properties a unique and remarkable world unto itself—a never-ending stage production that guests become a part of. According to the vice president of the Ritz-Carlton Leadership Center, Diana Orek, "Great service is about the people, the physical plant and the five senses. These three elements must work together to create an atmosphere that enhances the surrounding and, consequently, heightens the customer's experience. It's important to choose elements—sounds, visuals, tastes and smells—that harmonize with the backdrop. For example, having classical harp music playing in our public areas at The Ritz-Carlton, South Beach in Florida would be out of place. South Beach has a very vibrant, Latin/salsa vibe. So salsa music would better fit the atmosphere—the scenography—of The Ritz-Carlton, South Beach."[4]

This sense of total sensorial *engagement* works for Ritz-Carlton, and it's a principle that can and should be applied to all consumer situations. Any business—whether a 200,000-square-foot department store or a two-thousand-square foot independent shop—can and should create a unique and special sense of place that engages customers on every sensory level. What your customers smell, see, hear, touch and even taste inside your store should engage every neuron of their being.

Ritz-Carlton also ensures that its experiences stand out as *unique* relative to other hotels. It does this by changing the script guests would typically associate with hotel stays. Everything from the check-in through to housekeeping is done in a manner wholly unique to Ritz-Carlton. In fact, the chain became known for the very scripted language used by staff. For example, instead of saying "You're welcome" when thanked, hotel staff were instructed to respond with "It's my pleasure." They never used the word "but," instead saying "however." Ritz-Carlton recognized that a guest experience is merely the sum total of a number of smaller make-or-break moments throughout their stay. Every word exchanged with each staff member they encounter defines the moment. And each of those moments is an opportunity to delight a customer and to do so in a trademark fashion. At Ritz-Carlton, they sweat the small stuff.

More recently, the chain has allowed its employees to express themselves more freely while operating within these standards. To prevent the experience from feeling robotic or forced, "We've become intentionally less formal over time," says Herve Humler, president and chief operations officer. He explains, "We focus now on authentic, unscripted conversation and interactions with the customer. In the early days when putting together this hotel company and growing it globally, we scripted almost everything. You'd hear 'my pleasure' repeated everywhere you went in the hotel because that was part of the script. We have evolved from that today and now encourage our employees to be themselves. To conduct interactions with utmost respect and courtesy, but in a way that is natural to their personality and the warmth of their caring natures."[5]

Ritz-Carlton *personalizes* each guest's experience by having staff use their names whenever possible in conversation. They will remember details about the guest's stay—what outing they had planned for a particular day, for example, and then, when the guest returns, they may ask them how they enjoyed the tour, or shopping or whatever else they did. Staff are quick to take note of guest preferences and add those preferences to a central guest history file, accessible by all Ritz-Carlton properties. This extra gesture of remembering a guest's name, their plans and their preferences transforms an experience. Any retailer with a loyalty program should be leveraging that program—not only during the transaction but, most importantly, when the guest arrives in the shopping space, so that their needs, purchase history and preferences can be better catered to while they're there!

It's also typical to be pleasantly *surprised* by something while staying at a Ritz-Carlton hotel. In fact, staff are empowered to do just that. It may be something as small as having a unique treat sent up to your room—my wife and I, for example, returned to our room one evening to find an amazing little chocolate house had been left for us. Or it might be something larger. One of the company's policies permits employees to spend up to two thousand dollars per day to satisfy a single guest! I've heard anecdotes of this money being used for everything from buying a guest a new pair of nylons to one case in which a staff member flew to Cuba to purchase a unique box of cigars for an extremely loyal guest! Exceeding what your customers expect of you is the price to play. But the ability to deliver on what they didn't expect will create lifelong loyalty and love.

Moreover, Ritz-Carlton makes their experiences highly *repeatable* by building in strict but often unseen standards and service cues. One that I found amazing is that, when you order a glass of wine at a Ritz-Carlton, your glass will have a small lion logo etched on it, and the lion's tongue is sticking out. Don't take it personally! In fact, the lion's tongue indicates the fill-level for the staffperson pouring the wine. Not only does the staff member save Ritz-Carlton from the expense of over-pours, but the guest receives yet another perfectly uniform experience. When standards like this are applied across the thousands of activities that go into making a large hotel function, things appear to run seamlessly, creating a memorable and downright sublime customer experience.

> "Design is a funny word. Some
> people think design means how it looks.
> But of course, if you dig deeper,
> it's really how it works." **STEVE JOBS**

When all is said and done, though, the real art of executing the most highly engineered experiences is to make them look like they're *not* highly engineered. True mastery occurs when you can make the meticulous artistry and difficulty of something look effortless—an art Italians call *sprezzatura,* or studied carelessness. Achieving sprezzatura, however, is anything but effortless. It requires fanatical levels of design, training, practice and measurement. Great retailers are no different than the virtuoso pianist who seems to effortlessly crack off Chopin's famously difficult Opus 66, leaving onlookers oblivious to the thousands of hours of practice required to play at such a level of mastery. Truly fantastic retail experiences are as electrifying as an act of live theater, where the actors have so studied their parts as to become one with their characters.

Retail Is Alive

AND SO, WE COME full circle and, contrary to what Mark Andreessen, the media headlines or anyone else might tell you, retail is not dead. Not at all. It's merely shedding its skin. As we move into the post-digital era, the entire concept of retail will continue to transform before our eyes. And there will undoubtedly be winners and losers on both sides.

Today's solitary, antisocial and systems-driven approach to ecommerce will give way to the immersive, realistic and connected digital experiences of tomorrow, which will be almost indiscernible from reality. The drudgery of daily shopping trips for commodity goods will be almost entirely managed for us by networks of sensors and AI, allowing us more time to venture to the store for more inspired experiences. And with that, the staid and static physical stores we visit today will die off to make room for the dynamic and remarkable shopping spaces of the future: the places we go to learn, see, touch and play like never before. Experiences will be the most valuable products of the next century, and these experiences will engage our hearts, minds and bodies. These will be experiences so profound that we will, in many cases, pay just to browse! The entire economic model for retail will be rewritten: vendors will become clients and retailers will become skilled experiential media agencies, and both will become infinitely more successful and profitable than their predecessors.

This is the future of retail, and it's so bright you'll need sunglasses.

> "We all die. The goal isn't
> to live forever, the goal is to create something
> that will." CHUCK PALAHNIUK

In my journey toward mapping this future I discovered pioneering companies and individuals who, far from being the pallbearers at retailing's funeral, are the enthusiastic engineers of its reinvention. Some are reimagining the physical store, whereas others are training their skill and creativity on digital commerce. Still others are working to meld the two. Interestingly, many had no prior experience in retailing, which far from being an Achilles heel as was once believed, now seems to constitute a significant market advantage.

This influx of revolutionaries has brought with it a distinct culture shift in retail. Sometimes referred to as the accidental profession, retail, it seems, is becoming the chosen focus for savvy men and women coming out of schools such as Stanford, Cambridge and MIT. What's more, for the first time in a long time, retail is now regarded as a viable path for young, creative entrepreneurs who may not have an MBA or a degree of any kind, but who possess ingenuity, vision and drive. Retail has once again become an industry smart people are getting into... on purpose!

Regardless of their backgrounds, all of the people I spoke with for this book have been captivated by the clarion call of this historic turning point in humanity and commerce. Each of them sees unbounded potential in the future that lies ahead. Each of them is reengineering retail.

And if you can take one final thing from this book, I hope it's this: in the future, the only real certainty is that someone is going to completely reinvent what you do. What you need to determine now is whether that *someone* will be you.

Endnotes

CHAPTER 1

1 Sarah Lacy, "Andreessen Predicts the Death of Traditional Retail. Yes: Absolute Death," Pando.com, January 30, 2013, https://pando.com/2013/01/30/andreessen-predicts-the-death-of-traditional-retail-yes-absolute-death/.

CHAPTER 2

1 Shelly Banjo, "The End of an Era at Walmart," *BloombergGadfly*, March 31, 2016, https://www.bloomberg.com/gadfly/articles/2016-03-31/walmart-s-first-ever-sales-drop-marks-new-era.
2 Jason Ankeny, "Wal-Mart Reportedly in Negotiations to Acquire Jet," August 3, 2016, RetailDive.com, http://www.retaildive.com/news/wal-mart-reportedly-in-negotiations-to-acquire-jet/423789/.
3 Jillian D'Onfro, "Wal-Mart Is Losing the War against Amazon," *Business Insider*, July 25, 2015, http://www.businessinsider.com/wal-mart-ecommerce-vs-amazon-2015-7.
4 Phil Wahba, "This Chart Shows Just How Dominant Amazon Is," *Fortune*, November 6, 2015, http://fortune.com/2015/11/06/amazon-retailers-ecommerce/.

CHAPTER 3

1 Nick Wingfield, "Amazon's Cloud Business Lifts Its Profit to a Record," *The New York Times*, April 28, 2016, http://www.nytimes.com/2016/04/29/technology/amazon-q1-earnings.html?_r=0.

2 Amazon.com, "Amazon.com Announces Fourth Quarter Sales Up 22% to 35.7 Billion," press release, January 28, 2016, http://www.businesswire.com/news/home/20160128006357/en/Amazon.com-Announces-Fourth-Quarter-Sales-22-35.

3 Tonya Garcia, "Amazon Accounted for 60% of U.S. Online Sales Growth in 2015," MarketWatch.com, May 3, 2016, http://www.marketwatch.com/story/amazon-accounted-for-60-of-online-sales-growth-in-2015-2016-05-03.

4 Michael R. Levin, Consumer Intelligence Research Partners, "Amazon Prime Members Stay Members," June 1, 2016, updated June 7, 2016, http://www.huffingtonpost.com/michael-r-levin/amazon-prime-members-stay_b_10334678.html.

5 Krystina Gustafson, "The Fourth Biggest Retail Event Isn't Even a Holiday," CNBC.com, July 6, 2016, http://www.cnbc.com/2016/07/06/the-fourth-biggest-retail-event-isnt-even-a-holiday.html.

6 Nathan McAlone, "Amazon CEO Jeff Bezos Said Something about Prime Video that Should Scare Netflix," June 2, 2016, *Business Insider,* http://www.businessinsider.com/amazon-ceo-jeff-bezos-said-something-about-prime-video-that-should-scare-netflix-2016-6.

CHAPTER 4

1 Thad Rueter, "Global e-Commerce Sales Will Increase 22% This Year," *Internet Retailer,* December 23 2014, https://www.internetretailer.com/2014/12/23/global-e-commerce-will-increase-22-year.

2 Stefany Zaroban, "U.S. Ecommerce Grows 14.6% in 2015," *Internet Retailer,* February 17, 2016, https://www.internetretailer.com/2016/02/17/us-e-commerce-grows-146-2015.

3 U.S. Census Bureau, "Estimated Annual Sales of U.S. Retail and Food Services Firms by Kind of Business: 1992 through 2014," http://www.census.gov/svsd/retlann/pdf/sales.pdf.

4 "Nearly 70% of Americans Shop Online Regularly with Close to 50% Taking Advantage of Free Shipping," Mintel.com, July 13, 2015, http://www.mintel.com/press-centre/technology-press-centre/nearly-70-of-americans-shop-online-regularly-with-close-to-50-taking-advantage-of-free-shipping.

5 "eBay Inc. Reports Fourth Quarter and Full Year 2015 Results," *Business Wire,* January 27, 2016, http://www.businesswire.com/news/home/20160127006267/en/eBay-Reports-Fourth-Quarter-Full-Year-2015.

6 Vicky Huang, "Alibaba Passes $5 Billion in Singles' Day Sales in First Hour of Shopping," *The Street,* November 10, 2016, https://www.thestreet.com/story/13878121/1/alibaba-expects-to-deliver-big-on-singles-day-but-how-long-can-the-dominance-last.html.

7 Joe Tsai, "Joe Tsai Looks Beyond Alibaba's RMB 3 Trillion Milestone," *Alizila,* March 21, 2016, http://www.alizila.com/joe-tsai-beyond-alibabas-3-trillion-milestone/.

8 Sandrine Rastello, "China's E-Commerce Boom a Lesson for Creating Jobs in India," *Bloomberg Markets*, August 2, 2016, http://www.bloomberg.com/news/articles/2016-08-02/china-s-e-commerce-boom-a-lesson-for-creating-jobs-in-india.

9 Mary Meeker, Kleiner Perkins Caulfield Byers (KPCB), *Internet Trends Report: Code Conference*, June 1, 2016, http://www.kpcb.com/internet-trends.

10 Central Intelligence Agency (CIA), "Median Age," *The World Factbook*, 2015, https://www.cia.gov/library/publications/the-world-factbook/fields/2177.html.

11 "Online Retailing in India: The Great Race," *The Economist*, March 5, 2016, http://www.economist.com/news/briefing/21693921-next-15-years-india-will-see-more-people-come-online-any-other-country-e-commerce.

12 Erik Sherman, "Alibaba's IPO Filing: High Profits and Mystery," CBS News, May 7, 2014, http://www.cbsnews.com/news/alibaba-ipo-filing-high-profits-and-mystery/.

CHAPTER 5

1 "The Overcrowded Food-Delivery Industry," CB *Insights Blog*, August 1, 2016, https://www.cbinsights.com/blog/food-delivery-startups-crowded-market/.

2 Daniele Kucera, "Amazon Acquires Kiva Systems in Second-Biggest Takeover," *Bloomberg*, March 19, 2012, https://www.bloomberg.com/news/articles/2012-03-19/amazon-acquires-kiva-systems-in-second-biggest-takeover.

3 Deepa Seetheraman, "Amazon Rolls Out Kiva Robots for Holiday Season Onslaught," Reuters, December 1, 2014, http://www.reuters.com/article/amazoncom-kiva-idUSL3N0TL2U720141201.

4 Ananya Bhattacharya, "Amazon Is Just Beginning to Use Robots in Its Warehouses and They're Already Making a Huge Difference," *Quartz*, June 17, 2016, http://qz.com/709541/amazon-is-just-beginning-to-use-robots-in-its-warehouses-and-theyre-already-making-a-huge-difference/.

5 Scott Galloway, "Why Uber Is Set to Disrupt Amazon (and Other Tech Trends), *OpenView*, http://labs.openviewpartners.com/scott-galloway-amazon-facebook-google-apple-disruption/#.wBboKRS9fww.

6 Spencer Soper, "More Than 50% of Shoppers Turn First to Amazon in Product Search," Bloomberg, September 27, 2016, https://www.bloomberg.com/news/articles/2016-09-27/more-than-50-of-shoppers-turn-first-to-amazon-in-product-search.

7 Cindy Liu, *Worldwide Retail Ecommerce Sales: eMarketer's Updated Estimates and Forecast through 2019*, December 2015. See executive summary at https://www.emarketer.com/Report/Worldwide-Retail-Ecommerce-Sales-eMarketers-Updated-Estimates-Forecast-Through-2019/2001716.

8 Jorij Abraham and Kitty Koelemeijer, *The Rise of Global Marketplaces: How to Compete and Prosper in the World of Amazon, Alibaba and Other Platforms* (Amsterdam: Ecommerce Foundation, June 2015).

CHAPTER 6

1 Peter Kafka, "You Are Still Watching a Staggering Amount of TV Every Day," *Recode,* June 27, 2016, http://www.recode.net/2016/6/27/12041028/tv-hours-per-week-nielsen.

2 John Plunkett, "TV Advertising Skipped by 86% of Viewers," *The Guardian,* August 24, 2010, https://www.theguardian.com/media/2010/aug/24/tv-advertising.

3 Thales S. Teixeira, "The Rising Cost of Consumer Attention: Why You Should Care, and What You Can Do about It" (working paper 14-055, Harvard Business School, Boston, January 17, 2014), http://www.economicsofattention.com/site/assets/files/1108/teixeira_t-_the_rising_cost_of_attention_working_paper-1.pdf.

4 Rick Porter, Olympics 2016 Ratings: Gap with London Narrows, Still Down Double Digits, *Screener,* August 18, 2016, http://tvbythenumbers.zap2it.com/more-tv-news/olympics-2016-ratings-gap-with-london-narrows-still-down-double-digits/.

5 JC Lupis, "The State of Traditional TV: Q2 2016 Update," *Marketing Charts,* July 16, 2016, http://www.marketingcharts.com/television/are-young-people-watching-less-tv-24817/.

6 Leo Barraclough, "Global Advertising Spend to Rise 4.6% to $579 Billion in 2016," *Variety,* March 21, 2016, http://variety.com/2016/digital/global/global-advertising-spend-rise-2016-1201735023/.

7 "Social Network Ad Spending to Hit $23.68 Billion Worldwide in 2015," *eMarketer,* April 15, 2015, http://www.emarketer.com/Article/Social-Network-Ad-Spending-Hit-2368-Billion-Worldwide-2015/1012357.

8 Mark Ritson, Ritson vs Social Media, YouTube, January 7, 2015, https://www.youtube.com/watch?v=S2NUayn2vP0.

9 Justin Lafferty, "Forrester's Nate Elliott: There's No 'Community Building' on Social," *AdWeek,* June 4, 2015, http://www.adweek.com/socialtimes/forresters-nate-elliott-theres-no-community-building-on-social/621311.

10 Sahil Patel, "85 Percent of Facebook Video Is Watched without Sound," *Digiday,* May 17, 2016, http://digiday.com/platforms/silent-world-facebook-video/.

11 i100 staff, "Why Do People Use Social Media?," June 3, 2015, https://www.indy100.com/article/why-do-people-use-social-media-we-have-the-answers--bkBxB86Txl. The source data is from Deloitte.

12 Mark Sweney, "More than 9 Million Britons Now Use Adblockers," *The Guardian,* March 1, 2016, https://www.theguardian.com/media/2016/mar/01/more-than-nine-million-brits-now-use-adblockers.

13 Gerd Leonhard, in conversation with the author, March, 2013.

14 E.J. Schultz, "PepsiCo Exec Has Tough Words for Agencies," *Advertising Age,* October 15, 2015, http://adage.com/article/special-report-ana-annual-meeting-2015/agencies-fire-ana-convention/300942/.

CHAPTER 7

1 Satish Meena, *Forrester Research World Mobile and Smartphone Adoption Forecast, 2015 to 2020 (Global),* (Cambridge, MA: Forrester Research, September 24, 2015), https://www.forrester.com/report/Forrester+Research+World+Mobile+And+Smartphone+Adoption+Forecast+2015+To+2020+Global/-/E-RES127942.

2 Matt Lawson, "Win Every Micro-Moment with a Better Mobile Strategy," *think with Google,* September 2015, https://www.thinkwithgoogle.com/articles/win-every-micromoment-with-better-mobile-strategy.html.

3 Stacey MacNaught, "Tecmark Survey Finds Average User Picks Up Their Smartphone 221 Times a Day," *Tecmark,* 2014, http://www.tecmark.co.uk/smartphone-usage-data-uk-2014/.

4 Winston Churchill, "The Bright Gleam of Victory" (speech given at the Lord Mayor's Day Luncheon at the Mansion House, London, November 10, 1942), http://www.winstonchurchill.org/resources/speeches/1941-1945-war-leader/the-end-of-the-beginning.

CHAPTER 8

1 Dave Evans, *The Internet of Things: How the Next Evolution of the Internet Is Changing Everything,* White Paper (San Jose, CA: Cisco Internet Business Solutions Group, April 2011), 3, http://www.cisco.com/c/dam/en_us/about/ac79/docs/innov/IoT_IBSG_0411FINAL.pdf.

2 Jonathan Vanian, "Ignore the Internet of Things at Your Own Risk," Fortune.com, November 2, 2015, http://fortune.com/2015/11/02/internet-of-things-irrelevant/.

CHAPTER 9

1 Chris Messina, blog post of January 19, 2016, https://medium.com/chris-messina/2016-will-be-the-year-of-conversational-commerce-1586e85e3991#.i0gyfuc70.

2 Yongdong Wang, "Your Next New Best Friend Might Be a Robot," *Nautilus,* February 4, 2016, http://nautil.us/issue/33/attraction/your-next-new-best-friend-might-be-a-robot.

3 Marcelo Ballve, "Messaging Apps Are Overtaking Social Networks to Become the Dominant Platforms on Phones," *Business Insider,* April 10, 2015, http://www.businessinsider.com/messaging-apps-have-completely-overtaken-social-networks-to-become-the-dominant-platforms-on-phones-2015-4.

4 Khari Johnson, "Facebook Messenger Now Has 11,000 Chatbots for You to Try," *VentureBeat,* June 30, 2016, http://venturebeat.com/2016/06/30/facebook-messenger-now-has-11000-chatbots-for-you-to-try/.

5   Samuel Gibbs, "Now Anyone Can Build Their Own Version of Microsoft's Racist, Sexist Chatbot Tay," *The Guardian,* March 31, 2016, https://www.theguardian.com/technology/2016/mar/31/now-anyone-can-build-own-version-microsoft-racist-sexist-chatbot-tay.

6   Amazon, "Amazon Introduces the Alexa Fund: $100 Million in Investments to Fuel Voice Technology Innovation," *Business Wire,* June 25, 2015, http://www.businesswire.com/news/home/20150625005704/en/Amazon-Introduces-Alexa-Fund-100-Million-Investments.

7   Lucie Green, "Frontier(less) Retail," *SlideShare,* June 14, 2016, http://www.slideshare.net/jwtintelligence/frontierless-retail-executive-summary.

CHAPTER 10

1   Mark Zuckerberg's Facebook page, March 25, 2014, https://www.facebook.com/zuck/posts/10101319050523971.

2   Aliya Ram, "UK Retailers Count the Cost of Returns," *Financial Times,* January 27, 2016, https://www.ft.com/content/52d26de8-c0e6-11e5-846f-79b0e3d20eaf.

3   The Retail Equation, *2014 Consumer Returns in the Retail Industry* (Irvine, CA: The Retail Equation, December 2014), https://www.the retailequation.com/retailers/industryreports/pdfs/ir_2014_nrf_retail_returns_survey.pdf.

4   Amir Rubin, in conversation with the author, June 2016.

5   Ibid.

6   Beck Besecker, in conversation with the author, June 2016.

7   Shawn Brady, "Are You Ready for a New Sensation?" *Philadelphia City Paper,* April 18, 2012, http://mycitypaper.com/Are-You-Ready-For-A-New-Sensation/.

8   "The Psychology of Smell," Fifthsense.org.uk, http://www.fifthsense.org.uk/psychology-and-smell/.

9   Nicola Twilley, "Will Smell Ever Come to Smartphones?" *The New Yorker,* April 27, 2016, http://www.newyorker.com/tech/elements/is-digital-smell-doomed.

CHAPTER 11

1   Brad Esposito, "Residents Are Pissed That Their Neighborhood Has Become a Pokémon Go Hot Spot," *BuzzFeed,* July 12, 2016, https://www.buzzfeed.com/bradesposito/pokemon-go-rhodes?utm_term=.nb4Gg03ML#.lwyvbNwrR.

2   Magic Leap, Inc., "Magic Leap Announces $793.5 Million in New Funding," *PR Newswire,* February 2, 2016, http://www.prnewswire.com/news-releases/magic-leap-announces-7935-million-in-new-funding-300213369.html.

3   Sean Hollister, "How Magic Leap Is Secretly Creating a New Alternate Reality," *Gizmodo,* November 19, 2014, http://gizmodo.com/how-magic-leap-is-secretly-creating-a-new-alternate-rea-1660441103.

4 "Magic Leap Will Allow You to Virtually Try On Clothes," *Fortune Tech* video, 1:28, July 12, 2016, http://fortune.com/video/2016/07/12/magic-leap-mixed-reality/.
5 Romney Evans, in conversation with the author, June 2016.
6 Ibid.

CHAPTER 12
1 Mitchell Menaker, in conversation with the author, July 2016.
2 Ibid.
3 Eric Sprunk cited in Mark Bain, "Nike's COO Thinks We Could Soon 3D Print Nike Sneakers at Home," October 6, 2015, Quartz, http://qz.com/518073/nikes-coo-thinks-we-could-soon-3d-print-nike-sneakers-at-home/.
4 Joseph DeSimone (chief executive officer of Carbon 3D), in conversation with the author, July 2016.
5 Ibid.
6 Ibid.
7 Ibid.

CHAPTER 14
1 Utpal Dholakia, Ph.D., "How Terrorist Attacks Influence Consumer Behaviors," *Psychology Today*, December 1, 2015, https://www.psychologytoday.com/blog/the-science-behind-behavior/201512/how-terrorist-attacks-influence-consumer-behaviors.
2 David A. Koski, "Enhancing Online Shopping Atmosphere," United States Patent application 20080091553, filed September 29, 2006, and published on April 17, 2008, https://www.google.ch/patents/US20080091553.
3 Jana Kasperkevic, "Why Warby Parker Opened a Retail Store," *Inc. Magazine,* May 21, 2013, http://www.inc.com/jana-kasperkevic/warby-parker-co-founder-why-we-opened-a-flagship-store.html.
4 Ibid.
5 Mark Walsh, "The Future of E-Commerce: Bricks and Mortar," *The Guardian,* January 30, 2016, https://www.theguardian.com/business/2016/jan/30/future-of-e-commerce-bricks-and-mortar.
6 Kim Bhasin, "Custom Suit Startup Indochino Wants More Physical Stores," *Bloomberg*, December 8, 2015, http://www.bloomberg.com/news/articles/2015-12-08/custom-suit-startup-indochino-wants-more-physical-stores.

CHAPTER 15
1 Ian MacKenzie, Chris Meyer and Steve Noble, "How Retailers Can Keep Up with Consumers," *McKinsey & Company,* October 2013, http://www.mckinsey.com/industries/retail/our-insights/how-retailers-can-keep-up-with-consumers.
2 Jeffrey Sparshott, "Congratulations, Class of 2015. You're the Most Indebted Ever (For Now)," *Wall Street Journal,* May 8, 2015, http://blogs.wsj.com/

economics/2015/05/08/congratulations-class-of-2015-youre-the-most-indebted-ever-for-now/.

3 Caelainn Barr and Shiv Malik, "Revealed: The 30-Year Economic Betrayal Dragging Down Generation Y's Income," *The Guardian*, March 7, 2016, https://www.theguardian.com/world/2016/mar/07/revealed-30-year-economic-betrayal-dragging-down-generation-y-income.

4 "89% of All UK Retail Sales Touch a Physical Store," *Verdict Retail*, July 18, 2016, http://www.verdictretail.com/89-of-all-uk-retail-sales-touch-a-physical-store/.

5 Christopher Donnelly and Renato Scaff, "Who Are the Millennial Shoppers? And What Do They Really Want?," *Outlook: Accenture's Journal of High Performance Business*, https://www.accenture.com/ca-en/insight-out-look-who-are-millennial-shoppers-what-do-they-really-want-retail.

6 Ibid.

7 Rebecca Harris, "How Retailers Can Win Over Millennial Shoppers (Survey)," *Marketing*, October 13, 2015, http://www.marketingmag.ca/consumer/how-retailers-can-win-over-millennial-shoppers-survey-159116. The data cited is from Shikatani Lacroix's study of U.S. shoppers.

CHAPTER 16

1 Sonos, "First Sonos Retail Flagship Brings Music Home to New York City," PR *Newswire*, July 12, 2016, http://www.prnewswire.com/news-releases/first-sonos-retail-flagship-brings-music-home-to-new-york-city-300296998.html.

2 Louis J. Prosperi, "The Imagineering Model: Applying Disney Theme Park Design Principles to Instructional Design," *Slideshare*, 2014, http://www.slideshare.net/louprosperi1/the-imagineeringmodel.

3 Elizabeth Spaulding and Christopher Perry, "Making It Personal: Rules for Success in Product Customization," Bain & Company, September 16, 2013, http://www.bain.com/publications/articles/making-it-personal-rules-for-success-in-product-customization.aspx.

4 Laith Murad, in conversation with the author, July 2016.

5 Ibid.

6 Dinah Eng, "Does Joy Help You Sell?" *Fortune*, December 30, 2015, http://fortune.com/2015/12/30/pirch-kitchen-bath-store-sales/.

7 Avery Hartmans, "Apple's Retail Boss Wants Apple Stores to Resemble 'Town Squares,'" *Business Insider*, August 19, 2016, http://www.businessinsider.com/angela-ahrendts-apple-stores-social-2016-8.

8 Alexandra Ilyashov, "This Retailer Is Killing It at 'Athleisure' but Wants to Kill the Term," *Refinery 29*, June 10, 2016, http://www.refinery29.com/2016/06/113523/bandier-gym-clothes-athletic-apparel.

9 Ipsos, "Consumers Share Positive and Negative Experiences Equally," press release, February 17, 2016, http://www.ipsos-na.com/news-polls/pressrelease.aspx?id=7144.

10 Maxie Schmidt-Subramanian with Harley Manning, Colin Campbell, Dylan Czarnecki, "The Business Impact of Customer Experience," Forrester Research, March 27, 2014, https://www.forrester.com/report/The+Business+Impact+Of+Customer+Experience+2014/-/E-RES113421. The Customer Experience Index is an annual benchmark of customer experience quality among large global brands.

11 Bruce Temkin, *The ROI of Customer Experience* (Waban, MA: Temkin Group, March 2012), http://temkingroup.com/research-reports/the-roi-of-customer-experience/.

12 Nathan Skid and David Hall, "How Toms Wins at Retail by Not (Only) Selling Shoes," *AdAge*, August 26, 2016, http://adage.com/videos/how-toms-shoes-wins-by-not-selling-shoes/1158.

13 Ibid.

CHAPTER 17

1 Nathalie Tadena, "More than Half of US Consumers Don't Want to Friend a Brand Online," *Wall Street Journal,* September 18, 2014, http://blogs.wsj.com/cmo/2014/09/18/more-than-half-of-us-consumers-dont-want-to-friend-a-brand-online/.

2 Bridget Dolan, in conversation with the author, August 2016.

3 Ibid.

4 Kasey Lobaugh, Jeff Simpson and Lockesh Ohri, *Navigating the New Digital Divide: Capitalizing on Digital Influence in Retail*, Deloitte Digital, 2015, https://www2.deloitte.com/content/dam/Deloitte/us/Documents/consumer-business/us-cb-navigating-the-new-digital-divide-v2-051315.pdf.

5 Brad Brown, "REI's Brad Brown on Mapping Customer Journey," National Retail Federation, YouTube, September 30, 2014, https://www.youtube.com/watch?v=Z_YIppV8Svg.

CHAPTER 18

1 Grocery Manufacturers Association with PWC, *2013 Financial Performance Report: Growth Strategies: Unlocking the Power of the Consumer* (Washington: GMA with PWC, 2013), 74, http://www.gmaonline.org/file-manager/GMA_Publications/2013_Financial_Performance_Report_Final1.pdf.

2 Phalguni Soni, "Prospects Look Upbeat for Nike's Direct-to-Consumer Channel Stores," *Market Realist,* September 22, 2015, http://marketrealist.com/2015/09/prospects-look-upbeat-for-nikes-direct-to-consumer-channel/.

3 Elizabeth A. Harris, "A Store with Media in Mind," *The New York Times,* March 14, 2014, http://www.nytimes.com/2014/03/15/business/a-store-with-media-in-mind.html?_r=0.

4 Ibid.

5 Nathan Skid, "Marketer's Playbook Video: The Future of Customer Experience," *AdAge*, August 2, 2016, http://adage.com/article/news/marketer-s-playbook-future-customer-experience/305279/.

6 Phil Wahba, "Apple Extends Lead in U.S. Top 10 Retailers By Sales Per Square Foot," *Fortune*, March 13, 2015, http://fortune.com/2015/03/13/apples-holiday-top-10-retailers-iphone/.

7 Liz Parks, "Real-Time R&D," National Retail Federation, August 2, 2016, https://nrf.com/news/real-time-rd.

8 Salesforce Research, *2015 Connected Shoppers Report* (San Francisco: Salesforce Research, 2015), https://www.salesforce.com/form/industries/retail-shopper-survey.jsp.

9 "Digital Impact on In-Store Shopping: Research Debunks Common Myths," Think with Google, October 2014, https://www.thinkwithgoogle.com/research-studies/digital-impact-on-in-store-shopping.html.

10 U.S. Bureau of Labor Statistics, "Occupational Employment and Wages Summary," economic news release, May 2015, http://www.bls.gov/news.release/ocwage.nr0.htm.

11 U.S. Department of Health and Human Services, "U.S. Federal Poverty Guidelines Used to Determine Financial Eligibility for Certain Federal Programs,", https://aspe.hhs.gov/poverty-guidelines.

12 Carl Benedikt Frey and Michael A. Osborne, "The Future of Employment: How Susceptible Are Jobs to Computerisation?" University of Oxford, September 17, 2013, http://www.oxfordmartin.ox.ac.uk/downloads/academic/The_Future_of_Employment.pdf.

CHAPTER 21

1 *Merriam-Webster's Learner's Dictionary*, s.v. "innovation," http://learnersdictionary.com/definition/innovation.

2 Gary Hamel and Nancy Tennant, "The 5 Requirements of a Truly Innovative Company," *Harvard Business Review*, April 27, 2015, https://hbr.org/2015/04/the-5-requirements-of-a-truly-innovative-company.

3 V.L. Dawson, Thomas D'Andrea, Rosalinda Affinito and Erik L. Westby, "Predicting Creative Behavior: A Reexamination of the Divergence between Traditional and Teacher-Defined Concepts of Creativity," *Creativity Research Journal,* vol. 12, no. 1 (1999), 57-66, doi: http://dx.doi.org/10.1207/s15326934crj1201_7, http://www.tandfonline.com/doi/abs/10.1207/s15326934crj1201_7.

4 *Merriam-Webster's Collegiate Dictionary*, 11th ed., s.v. "iteration," http://www.merriam-webster.com/dictionary/iteration.

5 Elizabeth Blair, "More Than 50 Years of Putting Kids' Creativity to the Test," NPR, April 17, 2013, http://www.npr.org/2013/04/17/177040995/more-than-50-years-of-putting-kids-creativity-to-the-test.

6 Sir Ken Robinson cited in Marvin Bartel, "Stereotypes and Divergent Thinking," in Goshen College personal pages, https://people.goshen.edu/~marvinpb/11-13-01/Effects-of-Stereotypes.html.

7 Jonathan Rosenberg, "Jonathan Rosenberg: Rules to Success," YouTube, April 2, 2010, https://www.youtube.com/watch?v=P1T-1FqUBVY.

CHAPTER 22

1 Warren Berger, "The Power of 'Why?' and 'What If?'" *The New York Times,* July 2, 2016, http://www.nytimes.com/2016/07/03/jobs/the-power-of-why-and-what-if.html.

2 Jerry M. Burger, Joy Hornisher, Valerie E. Martin, Gary Newman, and Summer Pringle, "The Pique Technique: Overcoming Mindlessness or Shifting Heuristics?" Journal of Applied Social Psychology 37:9 (August 28, 2007), 2086-2096.

3 Lindsay Floryan, "Starbucks First Mover Advantage: Attacking the Mobile Payment Option," on Socials Cloud blog, February 18, 2012, accessed October 26, 2016, https://socialscloud.wordpress.com/2012/02/18/starbucks-first-mover-advantage-attacking-the-mobile-payment-option/.

CHAPTER 23

1 Astro Teller, "Google X Head on Moonshots: 10X Is Easier Than 10 Percent," *Wired*, February 11, 2013, https://www.wired.com/2013/02/moonshots-matter-heres-how-to-make-them-happen/.

2 James Allen, "Founder's Mentality® and the Paths to Sustainable Growth," Bain video, 18:46, September 9, 2014, http://www.bain.com/publications/articles/what-is-founders-mentality-video.aspx.

3 Allen Webb, "Starbucks' Quest for Healthy Growth: An Interview with Howard Schultz," *McKinsey & Company,* March 2011, http://www.mckinsey.com/global-themes/employment-and-growth/starbucks-quest-for-healthy-growth-an-interview-with-howard-schultz.

4 Ibid.

5 Steve Jobs, "Steve Jobs Insult Response," 1997 Worldwide Developers Conference, YouTube, https://www.youtube.com/watch?v=FF-tKLISfPE.

CHAPTER 24

1 Hamel and Tennant, "The 5 Requirements of a Truly Innovative Company."

2 Smith+Co, *A Few Tips on... Designing Your Customer Experience* (London: Smith+Co, 2013), http://www.smithcoconsultancy.com/pdfs/uploads/Customer_experience_design.pdf.

3 Michael Eagan, "What Is Scenography: The Origins of Stage Design through Architecture," ArtsAlive.ca, http://www.artsalive.ca/collections/imagined-spaces/index.php/en/learn-about/scenography.

4 Diana Orek, "Dear Ritz-Carlton: What Is Scenography, And How Does It Impact Customer Service?," The Ritz-Carlton Leadership Center blog, April 13, 2015, http://ritzcarltonleadershipcenter.com/2015/04/dear-ritz-carlton-what-is-scenography/.

5 Micah Solomon," Your Customer Service Is Your Branding: The Ritz-Carlton Case Study," *Forbes,* September 24, 2015, http://www.forbes.com/sites/micahsolomon/2015/09/24/your-customer-service-style-is-your-brand-the-ritz-carlton-case-study/#1cd4b9501b8a.

Credits

26 Jack Ma is the chairman of Alibaba International. Quoted in Sonia Kole-snikov-Jessop, "Spotlight: Jack Ma, co-founder of Alibaba.com," *New York Times,* January 5, 2007, http://www.nytimes.com/2007/01/05/business/worldbusiness/05iht-wbspot06.4109874.html.

70 Ray Kurzweil is an author/inventor. Quoted in an interview with Paul Solman as reported in "Ray Kurzweil: As Humans and Computers Merge . . . Immortality?" Singularity weblog, July 12, 2012, https://www.singularity-weblog.com/ray-kurzweil-pbs-immortality/.

190 Pascal Morand is the executive president of the Fédération Française de la Couture. See Pascal Morand, "What 3D Printing Means for Fashion," *Busi-ness of Fashion,* July 27, 2016, https://www.businessoffashion.com/articles/opinion/3d-printing-technology-disrupt-fashion-and-luxury-pascal-morand.

124 Mindy Grossman is the chief executive officer of the Home Shopping Network. Quoted in Cathleen Medwick, "Homing Instincts," *O, The Oprah Magazine,* June 2008, http://www.oprah.com/home/Decorating-Your-Dreamhouse.

143 William Gibson is a novelist and essayist. Quoted in "Books of the Year," *The Economist,* December 4, 2003.

167 Angela Ahrendts is the senior vice president of retail at Apple Inc. Quoted in Nick Statt, "Apple Just Revealed the Future of Its Retail Stores," *The Verge,* May 19, 2016, http://www.theverge.com/2016/5/19/11715726/apple-flagship-store-opening-san-francisco-photos.

210 George Blankenship is a former executive at Tesla, Apple and GAP Inc. Quoted from a conversation with the author, August 2016.

224 Lucie Greene is the worldwide director of the Innovation Group at J. Walter Thompson Intelligence. Quoted in Rachel Arthur, "Future of Retail: Artificial Intelligence and Virtual Reality Have Big Roles to Play," *Forbes,* June 15, 2016, http://www.forbes.com/sites/rachelarthur/2016/06/15/future-of-retail-artificial-intelligence-and-virtual-reality-have-big-roles-to-play/#34709ef5420c.

226 Miles Davis was a musician. This quote is popularly attributed to him.

232 James Bertrand was an artist. This quote is widely attributed to him.

239 Darren David and Nathan Moody are the chief executive officer and the design director, respectively, of Stimulant. See "San Francisco 6 Best Practices for Designing Experiences in Public Spaces," *HOW Design,* March 12, 2015, http://www.howdesign.com/featured-design-news/experience-design-public-spaces/.

242 Elon Musk is Tesla's chief executive officer. Quoted in an interview with Rohan Silva at Silicon Valley Comes to the UK roundtable event, November 15, 2012.

252 Steve Jobs was the co-founder of Apple Inc. Quoted in Gary Wolf, "Steve Jobs: The Next Insanely Great Thing," *Wired,* February 1, 1996, https://www.wired.com/1996/02/jobs-2/.

254 Chuck Palahniuk is a novelist. From *Diary: A Novel* (New York: Anchor Books, 2004).

Index

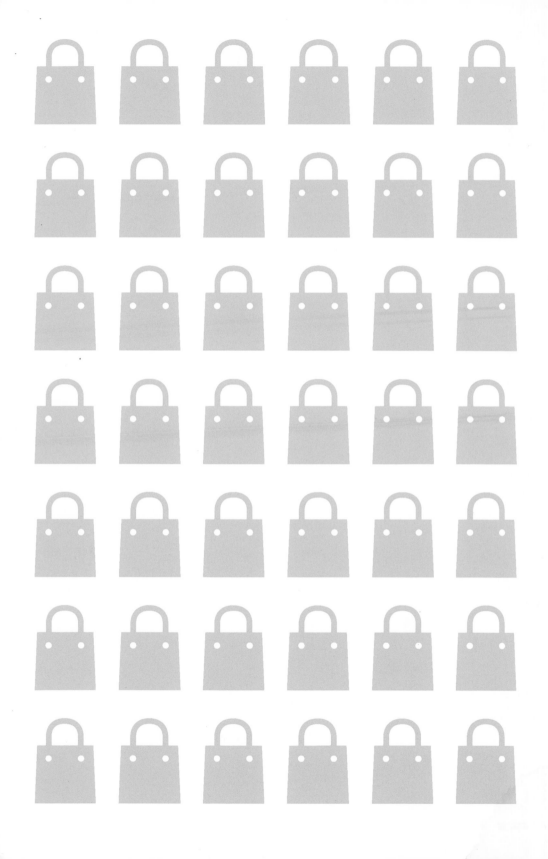

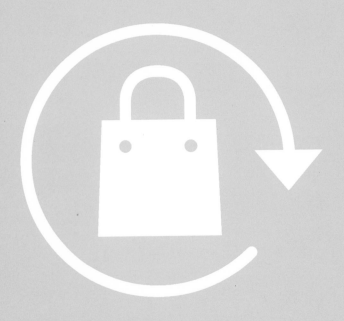